MAKING THE "TERRIBLE" TWOS TERRIFIC!

Other Books by John Rosemond

John Rosemond's Six-Point Plan for Raising Happy, Healthy Children

Ending the Homework Hassle: Understanding, Preventing, and Solving School Performance Problems

Parent Power! A Common-Sense Approach to Parenting in the '90s and Beyond

MAKING THE "TERRIBLE" TWOS TERRIFIC!

John Rosemond

**Andrews McMeel
Publishing, LLC**
Kansas City

09 10 RDC 24 23 22 21 20

Library of Congress Cataloging-in-Publication Data

Rosemond, John K., 1947—
    Making the terrible twos terrific / John Rosemond.
      p. cm.
    Includes index.
    ISBN-13: 978-0-8362-2811-3
    ISBN-10: 0-8362-2811-1
    1. Toddlers. 2. Child rearing. I. Title.
HQ774.5.R68 1993
649'.122—dc20

                             93-24948
                               CIP

Designed by Barrie Maguire

A Singing Dedication

To all the twos
I've known before,
and those that have yet
to be born;
in lieu of loving looks
I dedicate this book
to all the twos I've known before.

Acknowledgments

My heartfelt thanks to . . .

—Everyone at *The Charlotte Observer,* the Knight-Ridder Wire, *Better Homes and Gardens,* and Pace Communications (publishers of *Hemispheres,* the United Air Lines in-flight magazine), for their steadfast support and encouragement over the years.

—Becky Stout, director of the Providence Baptist Church Child Development Center (Charlotte, North Carolina), her staff, and especially the teachers in the two-year-old program, the parents of two-year-olds in the program, and the children themselves, for giving so generously of their time and teaching me so much in the process.

—Donna Martin and everyone at Andrews and McMeel, the best little publishing house in the whole wide world, for believing in me and cutting me so much slack.

—Willie, for believing in "the mission" enough to put up with the writing of another book.

—Beautiful Staniel Cay, Exuma, Bahamas, for being the best place in the whole wide universe in which to write a book.

—Eric and Amy, for their invaluable contributions of twenty-two and eighteen years ago, respectively.

Contents

Author's Note

Before you begin, I feel compelled to explain a few things:

—Concerning my selection of pronouns, when it is not awkward to do so, I use he/she or him/her. I have, however, found that constant use of the dual form is tedious; therefore, when the reference is arbitrary, I tend to use the male pronoun. When the reference is gender-specific, I employ whatever pronoun is appropriate. To those of you who interpret this policy as sexist, I would suggest that you not read the book, as your attention to, and irritation over, this detail is going to prevent you from ever getting "the big picture."

—In using the phrase "the twos," I am referring to that period in a child's life between eighteen and thirty-six months. These parameters, however, are nothing more than approximate, for "the twos" is not defined chronologically, but developmentally. In other words, the reference is not to an age, but to a set of developmental characteristics, the onset of which occurs, generally speaking, around eighteen months. Again speaking in general terms, it takes approximately eighteen months for this developmental stage to resolve itself. Please understand, however, that some children enter "the twos" earlier, some later. Likewise, the period of resolution varies from child to child, family to family.

—When you find me repeating myself, and you will, it is only because some of the issues, behaviors, and problems germane to a discussion of "the twos" are multifaceted. A certain behavior is described under more than one chapter heading when that behavior is relevant to more than one aspect of a two-year-old's development.

Introduction: A Reminiscence

The "terrible" twos? Ah, yes, I remember it well. The memory, starring the one-and-only, inimitable Eric the Energetic, is still vivid. There's Eric, age two, getting into everything, using my favorite album as a frisbee, playing in his mother's makeup, eating soap, saying "No!" to any and all instructions (wimpy requests, actually) from us, screaming bloody murder whenever one of us said "No!" to him, and generally running amok while Willie and I chased, grabbed, spanked, yelled, screamed, and generally ran amok. To know Eric at twenty-four is to wonder if this is the same child who didn't sleep through the night until he was two-and-a-half years old. Could this be the same Eric who was known as either "Mr. Mad" or "Mr. Tough," depending on his mood, by two of our best friends? Twenty-two years ago no one could have convinced me Eric would be sane when he grew up, much less the sensitive, thoughtful, responsible person he is today. (Eric graduated from North Carolina State University in May 1992, with a degree in economics, is employed as a commercial pilot, and was married to Nancy, the daughter-in-law of my dreams, in November 1992.)

It took another child, Amy, for Willie and me to learn that the "twos" can be a terrific time for both parents and child. There's no question about it, the reputation twos have for terribleness has, to some extent, been earned. But the difference—terrible or terrific—is not, we discovered, primarily a matter of child. It's a matter of parents.

This book is about the most dramatic and significant of all transitions in the development of a human being. Occurring between eighteen and thirty-six months (approximately), it is characterized by sweeping changes in the child's experience of both himself and the world. Needless to say, as the child's sense of who he is changes, so does the child's behavior. This much-maligned stage also has a somewhat deserved reputation for being one of the two most stressful periods in the parent-child relationship (the other occuring during the child's early adolescence), *but it doesn't have to be.*

The secret to transforming "terrible" into "terrific" is understanding—understanding the nature and course of the child's development during this critical stage; understanding that the behaviors associated with this transition are normal and, therefore, do not warrant overreaction; understanding that your role as parent is to bring about a necessary revolution in your child's way of perceiving and relating to the world; understanding that the typical two-year-old is not inclined to cooperate in this revolution; understanding that a loving, yet firm approach to discipline is the means of negotiating these potentially perilous developmental straits; understanding that you must discipline yourself in order to be effective at disciplining your child; understanding that any parental behavior that is driven by fear or frustration lacks discipline; understanding that this is the most precedent-setting of times in the parent-child relationship; understanding that you choose the precedents that are set; understanding that if you negotiate the challenges of this all-important developmental stage with skill and confidence, things will never get this bad again. Ever.

I wrote this book because Willie and I understood nothing the first time around, and it got ugly. We understood almost everything the second time around and it was a breeze (slight exaggeration). Understanding made the difference. So I wrote this book to help you understand, and with understanding, become a permanently successful parent, able to help your child become a permanently successful human being.

This is the book Willie and I needed when Eric was a toddler. It is based primarily on personal experience, which twenty-two years of professional experience has simply served to confirm. It was my intent to write a book that is low on theory and high on service, a book that is informative, enlightening, entertaining, and more than anything else, *useful.* If I succeeded, it is to Eric and Amy's credit; therefore, they join Willie and me in wishing you a creative, constructive, and most terrific time with your two-year-old!

Chapter 1

Understanding Your Two-Year-Old

*I*f it were possible to record and decode the burst of activity that occurs in the brain of a newborn child at the moment he first opens his eyes to behold the mysteries of the universe, the translation would likely read, "Wow! Look what I did!"

The newborn, lacking any other frame of reference, relates all early experience to himself, and himself alone. From his point of view, the world came into being at the moment he opened his eyes; therefore, the act of opening his eyes was the act of creation. It follows, from his point of view, that he reigns over all things, which exist for him and because of him. Amen.

"Egocentric" was the label Swiss developmental psychologist Jean Piaget (1896–1980) used to describe the infant's sense of omnipotent self-centeredness. This belief, that he is the source and center of all creation, is the child's first construction of reality. And for the first eighteen months or so of his life, his parents and other significant adults—if they are sensitive to his needs—respond to him *as if that belief were true.* When he's hungry, he signals to be fed, and someone feeds him. When he's tired of walking, he signals to be carried, and someone carries him. When he's alone and wants attention, he yells and someone appears, eager to do his bidding. And on an on it goes; whether uncomfortable, frustrated, or just plain bored, he pulls the strings, and his parents (and other responsible adults) cooperate. Add to this the fact that as he's being pushed through public places in his stroller, people are constantly approaching and kneeling in front of his portable throne, begging for the favor of a smile. Given the manner in which he is treated and responded to during his first eighteen months, he has every reason to believe he is El Magnifico Supremo, The First and Only One of Any True Importance Over Whose Illustrious Countenance the Sun Rises and Sets. Long before his eighteenth month, his very sense of security has come to rest upon the conclusion—arrived at honestly—that he rules the world. His psychological stability has come to depend, in other words, upon continued reinforcement/validation of that *egocentric* premise.

In the process of catering to his self-centered fantasies, his parents have established one abiding, all-important understanding: beyond any doubt, he can *trust* his parents (and their responsible, loving substitutes) to be there when he needs them. As we shall soon see, of all the features and psychological dimensions of the parent-child relationship that form during the first eighteen months of life, trust is the only one that will endure, that needs to endure. Trust provides the stability, the ballast the relationship will need to navigate the stormy seas that lie ahead.

Midway through the child's second year of life (or thereabouts), his parents initiate the process of "socialization"—the attempt to transform him from Cosmic Potentate into a responsible (and most uncosmic) member of society. Without warning, they begin refusing to cater to his every whim. They demand that he begin doing certain things for himself. They limit his freedom. They make him wait for things he wants, and even, on occasion, reject his demands completely and without explanation. In short order, they change the name of the game from "You're in Charge" to "We're in Charge." This effectively yanks the rug of his egocentric-based sense of security out from under him, lands him on his regal butt, and makes him completely and ferociously furious. How dare they!

Introducing . . . that most Terrible of Terribles, that most Furious of Furies, the one, the only (or so he continues to think), Two-Year-Old! Well, actually, he's not quite two, but we round up to the next highest number just to play a trick on parents who mistakenly think another six months or so of peace lie ahead. In response to this uprising, the toddler does exactly what anyone else would do if the rug of his security was suddenly jerked out from under him: he screams, refuses to cooperate or even negotiate with the leaders of the rebellion, and denies that they have the power to accomplish their aims. They say sit down, he stands up. They tell him to pick up his toys, he yells *"no!"* They refuse to pick him up on demand, he falls on the floor, flailing and screaming and foaming at the mouth. Someone tries to pick him up when he does not want picking up, and he gives them a "high five" to the nose.

The so-called "terribles," which last from eighteen to thirty-six months (give or take a few months on either side) are without question the most important time in the child's development, and the most important in the parent-child relationship, as well. It is during this critical eighteen-month period that parental authority is established; hopefully, that is. Keep in mind, however, that parental authority can only be constructed upon a firm foundation of *trust* laid during the first year and one-half of life. Without that foundation, chaos in the parent-child relationship will not only be inevitable, but indefinite in its duration. The outcome will be either a child who runs the show forever (anarchy), or parents who rule (always tentatively) by intimidation and force.

Taking It Apart

In order to establish that parents are in charge, it is necessary that the child's egocentricity—his first concept of how the world is organized and works, the foundation of his first sense of security—be slowly but surely dismantled. At this stage, his parents' primary job, their utmost responsibility, becomes that of erecting a fortress of authority that is, at first, all-encompassing —an authority that encircles the child, providing not only direction but protection as well and, as a result, guaranteeing the child's welfare. The cornerstone of that fortress becomes the cornerstone of a new and far more stable sense of security, one based upon the child's belief that his parents are the most powerful people in the known world, capable of providing for and protecting him under any and all circumstances. In effect, the parents' task is that of firmly yet gently convincing the child that he was mistaken—he does not rule the world, *they do.*

If his parents are successful, then by age three, the child "believes" in what Piaget termed the "omnipotency myth," the utterly absurd notion that his parents are all-powerful, all-seeing, all-knowing, all-capable. The All of All. Piaget (who, by the way, was the Einstein of child development in the twentieth century, and perhaps for all time) used to tell his students that parents are the child's first representation of God, a first and final powerfully loving (equal emphasis, please) authority. As the child grows toward adulthood, this concept mellows and transfers to other authority figures—teachers, lawmakers, ministers. Ever so gradually, it matures into an understanding that the universe is shaped and moved by a spiritual source/force beyond human comprehension—a source that is both infinitely powerful and infinitely loving/forgiving. This is the challenge that confronts the toddler's parents—to provide that model.

The irony of all this is that in order to help the toddler establish a sense of security that is based on the way things really are, his parents must first make him insecure—they must take his egocentric concept of how the world works and his place in it completely apart before they can help him put it back together in more mature form. Now, no child worth his mettle is going to take this lying down. This is revolution! This means war! And war it is, as the child fights to hold on to the only sense of security he's ever known while his parents slowly pry his fingers from the prize.

If the process turns out the way it should, if the child's parents are clear as to their task and proceed properly, then by age three (again, approximately) the child's egocentricity will have yielded to *parent-centricity*. He will now believe that his parents are the center of the known universe; that they are omnipotently capable of controlling a world he now realizes, intuitively, he cannot control on his own. This revision in his perception of the world is necessary to his becoming a responsible member of society. Moreover, it is essential to his successful emancipation. The only child who can move confidently *away* from his parents into an ever-increasing state of autonomy and self-sufficiency is a child who is completely secure in his parents' ability to care for him. The child whose parents have not succeeded in creating that security is a child who cannot move far away from them, who cannot explore, and therefore expand, the limits of his competence. Unconvinced of their ability to provide for him and protect him under any and all circumstances, he must remain close, dependent. And he will wallow without direction in this state of perpetual dependency until his parents resolve this issue, if ever they do so.

Putting It Back Together

It follows that if the young child needs to perceive his parents as powerful people, his parents have a responsibility to exercise power *responsibly* (the operative word) in his life. Their power secures his existence and, in so doing, enables the growth of independence and self-competence.

It occurs to me that the age-old children's game of "It" is nothing more than a metaphorical representation of this dynamic. As you will no doubt recall, the game begins with one child in the group being chosen to be "It"—the embodiment of menace, threat. The children then designate a place as "Home"—a haven, a sanctuary where they are safe from the harm "It" represents. The idea, of course, is to venture as far away from "Home" as you can without being tagged by "It." At first, a child takes but a few tentative steps away before anxiety overwhelms him and he races back to safety. When the child reaches "Home"—as represented by a tree, perhaps—he may even throw his arms around it, trying to squeeze from it all the reassurance he can. As his courage builds, he ventures farther and farther away until he finally wins the game by breaking through the sphere of "It's" influence. At this point, he's free, emancipated.

The metaphor is all but obvious: In order to successfully emancipate himself, a child must be secure in his or her parents' power, as represented by their loving authority. The more effectively they communicate that authority, the more secure the child feels, and the better able he is to move away from them toward a life of his own. During this lengthy process, whenever he feels threatened, he turns back toward the safety of his parents' love and authority. In other words, it is impossible for a child to emancipate himself successfully unless he knows exactly where his parents *stand*, both literally and figuratively. That requires, of course, that his parents know where they themselves stand. If they don't know where they stand—if, in other words, they are insecure in their authority—they cannot communicate security to their child, and he cannot move successfully away from them. Under the circumstances, he will become clinging, or disobedient, or both.

Let us always keep in mind that a disobedient child is a child who is simply trying to pin his parents down. His parents stand in one place one moment, another place the next. That constant wavering forces the child to constantly test. Testing is nothing more than a desperate, misguided, no-win attempt on the part of a child to make his parents stand in one spot so that he can get on with his life's work of winning the game of "It."

The Benevolent Dictatorship

A journalist recently asked what I find to be the most common mistake parents make in the rearing of children. I answered, "Failing to make their children *believe* in them." This is the most important of all precedents in the parent-child relationship. The young child's security rests upon this one belief: that without a shadow of doubt, his parents are willing and able to protect him, provide for him, and guide him at all times and in all places. This requires that his parents convey to him an unquestionable sense of unconditional love and personal strength. In effect, his parents must become, in his eyes, *heroes*.

Most of us, I'm sure, can remember, as young children, being absolutely convinced that there was but one most beautiful mother and one strongest father: our own! No other child's parents were smarter or better at anything. This is the essence of Piaget's omnipotency myth. This childish mythology represents a *need* on the part of the child to have parents who fit that description. That mythology, therefore, defines one of a parent's primary responsibilities—the proper conveyance of loving authority.

This is accomplished not so much according to a certain set of methods as it is by a certain attitude, which, if pressed to define, I would say consists of equal parts tolerance, resolve, commitment, and patience, along with an understanding of how children develop. The methods, whatever they are, must be firm, but gentle. That is not to say spankings are ruled out, because the most effective spankings, as we will discuss later, fit that description to a T. The overall idea is not to make the child subservient, but to create for him an authority upon which he can rely.

When, in the late 1970s, I first began speaking on this subject, I referred to this sort of reliable parent as a "benevolent dictator." Some folks were shocked. Some were amused. Regardless, most misunderstood. I said "benevolent dictator," but they heard only "dictator." I remember quite a few people accusing me of "promoting parental tyranny." Not so. I was saying that a parent's two most important responsibilities are those of communicating unconditional love and unconditional authority; to be, in other words, a "benevolent dictator," in the truest sense of the term.

It's unfortunate that most people, when they hear the word "dictator," think in terms of historical evildoers like Adolph Hitler and Idi Amin. The root word of "dictator" is the word "dictate," which the dictionary defines thus: *to instruct or direct with authority.* Is there anyone out there who does not agree that it is a parent's responsibility to direct and instruct with authority—as if, in other words, we know what we want, what we are doing, and what we're talking about? I didn't think so. Therefore, in the strictest (no pun intended) sense of the term, parents are (or should be) *benevolent dictators.*

The job of parent is that of balancing love and authority such that one is lovingly authoritative as well as authoritatively loving. Parenting "experts" of the sixties and seventies—including psychologist Thomas Gordon, author of the highly influential *Parent Effectiveness Training (PET)*—said that parental authority damaged the self-esteem of children because it placed children in "one down" positions relative to their parents. Balderdash! Poppycock! Frog feathers! That opinion is a construction of misguided imagination. It is *not* a representation of reality. The reality is that a child's self-esteem is synonomous with security; that security is provided by parents who balance love and authority in their caring for the child; that a child's security/self-esteem is not disrupted by exercise of authority, but is disrupted when love and authority are not in balance—when, in other words, parents are either overindulgent (love without authority) or disapprovingly tyrannical (authority without love).

Please, please don't confuse the terms *authoritative* and *authoritarian.* Although they share the same root, they are as different as night and day. An *authoritative* parent is self-confident. An *authoritarian* parent is insecure. An *authoritative* parent accepts children for what they are. An *authoritarian* parent cannot accept children for what they are and is, therefore, threatened by their misbehavior, impulsivity, lack of tolerance for frustration, and so on. The authoritarian parent responds to this threat with verbal and physical aggression. This aggression is the vain (in both senses of the term) attempt to make the child conform to the parent's distorted image of what a "good" child ought to be.

The most opportune time for establishing the benevolent dictatorship is between eighteen and thirty-six months. Is it an easy thing to accomplish? No, but it is, nonetheless, absolutely necessary that you create it. How? By establishing three understandings:

The first of these is the understanding, communicated from parent to child, "I am the center of attention in *your* life, but you are no longer the center of attention in mine." In other words, the child is, from this point forward, to pay more attention to the parent than the parent pays to the child. When challenged on this point (as I often am), I simply ask the skeptic, "Who, in the parent-child relationship, is the role model?"

"The parent," the skeptic responds.

I then ask, "How is it possible for a parent to be an effective role model, to set a good example, to teach, unless the child is paying more attention to the parent than the parent is paying to the child?"

At this point, the open-minded skeptic will think for a moment, then respond, "It isn't." Case closed.

One of the most significant things I learned as a parent was this: *Children will not pay attention to adults who are acting as if it is their primary obligation to pay attention to those children.* In the mind of the child, it is either the job of adults to pay attention to him, or his to pay attention to adults. For the first eighteen months of life, it is absolutely necessary that adults create the impression that it's *their* job to pay attention to the child. As a result, young toddlers do not feel they are obligated to pay attention to their parents. This is why young toddlers run away from their parents in shopping centers and other public places, oblivious to the danger. They do not pay attention to their parents because, in their minds, it is their parents' responsibility to pay attention to them. Period. The next eighteen months is spent convincing the child otherwise. It boils down to this: It is the job of adults to teach. You cannot teach a student who isn't paying attention. Period.

The second of these understandings is, "You will do what I, your parent, tell you to do."

Upon hearing this bit of heresy, a woman in Austin, Texas, spoke up to complain that this rule failed to acknowledge that children had opinions. Wrong! An *authoritarian* parent refuses to accept that children have minds of their own. An *authoritative* parent not only accepts that fact, but celebrates it. In the Rosemond family, for example, Eric and Amy were always allowed to express their opinions. We encouraged discussion, even disagreement. But both children understood that while they were always free to disagree, they were not free to disobey. In other words, when all was said and done, my wife and I, taking the child's point of view into consideration, would make a decision. The decision, for better or worse, was binding. We accepted that our children would, in fact, occasionally disobey. When they did so, the penalty would have a negative impact upon their freedom. Therefore, they were not *free* to disobey.

A woman in Omaha: "But I'm not always sure I'm making the right decision."

Yours truly: "You may not always make the very best decision you could possibly make, but you will surely make a better decision for your child than he would have made for himself."

Woman in Omaha: "Then, if I later realize I've made a bad decision, I shouldn't apologize or change my mind?"

Yours truly: "The only parent who, upon realizing a bad decision has been made, cannot apologize or change his or her mind, is an insecure parent. Authoritative parents are not insecure."

I hope that clears up whatever misunderstandings may have been forming in your mind up until this point.

The last of these three understandings follows upon the second. It might be stated thus: "You will do what I say not because I am successful at persuading you of the rightness of my point of view, not because I entice you to cooperate with an attractive-enough bribe, not because I threaten to hurt you if you don't, but *because I say so.*"

Old-fashioned? If, by that, you mean traditional, then yes, old-fashioned it is. "Because I said so" is an attitude that accepts two realities: First, most of a parent's decisions, rules, whatever, are founded on nothing more substantial than personal preference. They are, in the language of the jurist, arbitrary and capricious. You draw the figurative "line" where your personal comfort ends and your discomfort begins. Your child goes to bed at eight o'clock not so much because he *needs* a certain amount of sleep, but because you become uncomfortable (impatient, irritable, claustrophobic) when he stays up past eight o'clock. Your child cannot ride his bicycle past the corner because you become uncomfortable (anxious, fearful) when he ventures past that point. There is nothing perfectly "right" about an eight o'clock bedtime or not riding bicycles farther than the nearest corner. They are functions of parental comfort levels. That is why two different parents with two different comfort levels have different rules. The arbitrariness of our rules becomes apparent every time our children tell us that all their friends can stay up past eight o'clock and ride their bikes onto the next block.

The second reality reflected in "because I said so" is this: any and all attempts to "reason" with young children are fruitless. *A child cannot understand an adult point of view.* (Please read that again, out loud.) *A child will understand an adult point of view when the child is an adult.* (Again, read out loud.) Therefore, your child does what you say not because you are persuasive, but because you say so.

Does this mean you should never tell a child the reasons behind your decisions? No. It simply means you make no attempt to *reason*; no attempt, in other words, to persuade the child that your reasons are right, good, in his best interests, holy, pure, or whatever. You give your reasons knowing fully that the child will not agree with them. You give your reasons in order to provide the child with a reference point. Later, when the child is an adult, this reference point will be indispensable. In the meantime, understanding that like fine wine, no *mind* matures before its time, you do not expect agreement from a child concerning your adult point of view; therefore, you are not disappointed when the child does not agree. Because you are not disappointed, you are not upset when the child demonstrates his or her disagreement. You stay calm, and as such, are able to communicate to the child that you know where you stand, and furthermore, you know where you want him to stand. He may not, at the moment, like it. In the long run, however (and believe me on this), he will come to appreciate it and love and respect you all the more for it.

These three understandings, which compose an attitude of benevolent dictation, need to be communicated during the second eighteen months of life. If you push any sooner at this process, you run the risk of disrupting the establishment of trust. If you wait too long, you will find yourself having to paddle back upstream concerning the establishment of your authority. In child rearing, as in comedy, timing is everything.

The Malevolent Dictator?

"You know what disturbs me about your message?" she asked, she being a woman who had just heard me speak in Tallahassee.

"I haven't a clue," I answered.

"When you talked about your three understandings—you know, that stuff about the parent being the center of attention and the child doing what he's told because the parents tell him to do it—you never once mentioned the word *love*."

I reflected upon this a moment, then said, "You're right. I never actually said the word 'love.' What does that omission mean to you?"

"I interpret that to mean you lack a certain sensitivity to the emotional needs of children," she replied.

This woman came by her misjudgment honestly. Those three understandings, part and parcel of every pre–World War II generation's management of children, were branded as heretical, even abusive, by a current generation of professionals hell-bent on convincing us we were all raised in horribly dysfunctional families (see the writings of John Bradshaw, for example) and, therefore, are all in need of—guess what?—*therapy,* which those same supposedly altruistic professionals are willing to provide for upward of eighty dollars an hour. Notwithstanding the avalanche of psycho-babble descending upon us from many corners of the professional community these days, those three understandings are the very essence of a creative, loving parent-child relationship.

In the absence of those three understandings, it is impossible for a child to know where a parent stands. The absence of those understandings, in fact, generally means the parent is looking to the child for indication of where to stand. A child who does not know where his parent stands must test, test, test, test, test, ad infinitum. The child has no other choice. As I said earlier, constant testing is the attempt on the part of a child to pin a parent down. Here is an indisputable fact: *Testing raises the level of stress and tension in the parent-child relationship, thus obstructing the flow of affection and creative communication.* The way to minimize testing is to communicate to the child, "I know where I stand, and I know where I want you to stand." Under these circumstances, the child will test for only a short period of time, then stop. The resulting lack of stress between parent and child releases the full potential for affection in the relationship. So, you want a loving relationship with your child? Then you have no choice other than to communicate to him that, first, you are the center of attention in his life; second, he will do what you say; third, because you say so.

One reason people have difficulty accepting these three "benevolently dictatorial" understandings is because the professional community, beginning some forty years ago, encouraged us to approach the rearing of children as if it were an intellectual challenge, rather than a matter of common sense. Let me point out simply that if intellect was key to successful child rearing, the smartest people would be the best parents. That is hardly consistent with my observations.

An intellectual approach to child rearing is likely to result in the perception that child rearing is difficult, as in "the hardest thing I've ever done," a complaint I hear from many parents. Consider this: Ours is the first generation of American parents to make this complaint. Consider this: Ours is the only culture on the planet making this complaint. Conclusion: There is nothing about the rearing of children that is inherently difficult, but there must be something in our American approach (postwar) to child rearing that creates the illusion of difficulty. That something, I submit, is an overload of intellect, along with a corresponding paucity of common sense.

If you bring too much intellect to the child-rearing process, you will analyze your own behavior and the behavior of your child to neurotic excess, you will question yourself and your decisions constantly, you will waffle and waver and consume yourself with anxiety. In so doing, you will fail to communicate to your child that you know where you stand and know where you want him or her to stand. Your child will be forced to test compulsively. The level of stress in the relationship will rise, and the constant rocking of your household's "ship of state" will threaten your child's security and, therefore, self-esteem. A commonsensical approach to child rearing is not, by any means, unthinking. It is simply unintellectual. Common sense comes from the heart and the gut, not from the head. When a parent thinks too much, the heart becomes confused. When the heart rules, the head thinks clearly.

Perhaps it would further clarify the commonsensical nature of these three understandings if I pointed out that they also mediate the relationship between teacher and child in the classroom.

The First Understanding: Any good teacher knows you cannot effectively teach a child unless you command the child's attention. A teacher who fails to position herself at the center of her students' attention is a teacher who does not know the first thing about teaching. Parents are teachers, too. Likewise, they can effectively teach only if they command their children's attention. By the way, the difference between *commanding* a child's attention and *demanding* it is night and day. In the first place, the former succeeds while the latter does not. Second, you *command* by projecting self-confidence, as in you know where you stand, and you know where you want the child to stand. Adults who *demand* the attention of children do not know how to command it. Their demands are symptoms of insecurity.

The Second Understanding: All good teachers tell their students what to do and expect them to do it. If there is resistance, they enforce their expectations calmly, but firmly. There is no "I wish you would" in the way good teachers communicate expectations to children. They communicate in terms of "you will," period.

The Third Understanding: If a child is so bold as to challenge a teacher's expectations, the teacher, if she knows her business, will not engage in debate with the child, but will simply say, "You will do these things *because I tell you to do them.*"

Now, no one is shocked when a teacher communicates and enforces these understandings. No one, furthermore, accuses her of not loving her students. In fact, because it is inevitable that her students demonstrate not only superior learning, but also great affection for her, this is the very teacher most likely to be cited as "Teacher of the Year." So, why then are some people shocked at the suggestion that these same understandings must apply in the home? Could it be they think too much?

Who's on First?

A Des Moines, Iowa, couple once asked me for "the key" to successful discipline of a two-year-old. I answered, "Pay more attention to your marriage than you do your child. Effective discipline flows from the fundamental understanding that the marriage is the most important relationship in the family, occupies center stage, and functions as 'ringmaster' in the family circus."

Discipline is not the sum of a set of methods. It is a climate of understanding that permeates every aspect of the family's life. Within the context of that understanding, methods become relatively arbitrary. Whether, when a child misbehaves, you pop his rear end or sit him in a chair or take away a privilege or simply give a stern look is of little consequence. What matters is that parents—or single parent, as the case may be—are the center of attention, and that they act decisively from that state of centeredness.

The unspoken understanding in the parent-child relationship should be (from parent to child), "When I want your attention, you have no choice but to give it to me, but when you want mine, I have a choice. If you truly need it, you will receive it. But if you only *want* my attention, and the wanting is whimsical, there's a distinct chance you will have to do without it."

Translate: "I am the center of your attention. You are not the center of mine."

During the first eighteen months of life or so, realities demand that the child be the center of attention in the family. Taking the child slowly but surely out of the center takes another eighteen months. That transition, embodied by the above understanding, defines the parent-child dynamic during the "twos." If the parents are successful at guiding the child through this transition, then from his third birthday onward, the child intuitively understands that he is expected to pay more attention to his parents than they pay to him. That acceptance is essential to his being able not only to respect his parents, but to learn from them. This essential understanding embodies the two most fundamental purposes of discipline: First, it is limit-setting in that it defines the limits of the child's access to the parent. If access is unlimited—if, in other words, the child is the center of the parent's attention—then, in the child's view, there are no limits to what he can demand and receive. Second, it promotes self-esteem. Making it clear, albeit unspoken, that the child is not a "member of the wedding" gives the child permission to become independent. He learns to stand on his own two feet, which is the essence of self-esteem.

When, in a two-parent family, the child becomes the center of attention, and the child's relationship with one or both parents consumes more energy than does the parents' relationship with one another (when, in other words, they are mother and father more than they are husband and wife), it becomes easy for the child to "divide and conquer." Parents can only act decisively if they act in unison.

In a single-parent family, it must be equally clear that the parent is neither friend nor sibling, and that his/her life does not revolve around the child. It must be established that the single parent has a life of his/her own, completely independent of child-rearing responsibilities. A parent cannot be indulgently devoted to a child and define limits effectively. Nor can a parent be in a position of "service" to a child and promote the steady growth of autonomy.

Self-Esteem:
What It Is, and What It Isn't

Prior to World War II, if you were a young parent and met with some difficulty in the course of rearing a child, you didn't take yourself or your child to a therapist of one sort or another. Instead, you took your problem to your mother, your grandmother, or an older family friend. These folks gave advice that was based on lives they had led. It was rooted in the soil of common sense, it was practical, and it was reassuring.

In the aftermath of the war, extended family clusters began breaking up into nuclear family units that fanned out across the

country, each seeking its own slice of the new "American dream."
As a result, extended-family supports became less available to
new parents. To fill the void, we began handing over to the professional community—more specifically, to so-called "helping
professionals"—the responsibility of *informing* new parents, of
helping them find their balance.

By and large, however, professionals dispensed advice based
not on lives they had led, but on books they had read. Their perspective had been shaped less by real-life experience and more
by an academic one. Their advice was, therefore, more intellectual than commonsensical, more abstract than down to earth.

The professional perspective transformed our cultural out-
look on the raising of children. Previous generations felt that a
parent's most fundamental aim was the teaching of respect, responsibility, and resourcefulness—what I call the "Three R's of
Child Rearing." If you succeeded at endowing your children
with the Three R's, your child-rearing skills were held in high
regard by your peers. By the early seventies, however, the professional community had succeeded in convincing parents that
their primary task was that of seeing to it that their children
developed something they called *good self-esteem.*

Self-esteem became the buzzword of "parenting" in the seventies and has retained that coveted status ever since. For twenty
years or more, the professional community has told American
parents their first obligation is to promote and protect this neb-
ulous psychological entity. That same professional community
created the impression that self-esteem is something adults be-
stow upon children by giving them an abundance of attention
and praise. The more of those things you give your kids, the "experts" said, the better they will feel about themselves and the
better their self-esteem (read: the happier they) will be.

In effect, the "experts" implied that any parental decision that
made a child unhappy was likely to result in loss of self-esteem.
So, wanting only the best for their children, American parents
dedicated themselves to making, and keeping, their children
happy. The American child was allowed to occupy center stage
in the family, was deferred to on matters of family policy, and
was the recipient of a disproportionate percentage of the family's discretionary income.

It is, therefore, hardly surprising that a good number of people express concern that my philosophy of child rearing seems inconsistent with the tenets of the *nouveau* self-esteem theory. But self-esteem is not something bestowed upon children. It is something children work toward and discover for themselves. It is not something given to children by doting parents. It is earned, as are all truly valuable things. It does not grow in direct proportion to the amount of effort parents put into praising and doing things for children, or giving them attention. It grows as children learn to do for themselves.

We have forgotten what Thomas Jefferson told us in 1776: that we are endowed by the Creator "with certain unalienable Rights, that among these are Life, Liberty and the Pursuit of Happiness." Not happiness, mind you, but its *pursuit.* By implication, Jefferson warned that if you pursue happiness for someone else, you deny him the right to pursue it on his own.

Jefferson was right. You cannot "make" self-esteem in a child's life. You can only create opportunity for its discovery. Growth in self-esteem takes place as the child realizes that despite initial anxieties, frustrations, fears, even failures, he is capable of standing on his own two feet and dealing squarely with the challenges of living. The road to that discovery is paved not by parents running ahead of the child, making sure he encounters nothing but positive experiences along the way, but by parents who have the courage and common sense to "make" a good amount of reality in his life.

I spend most of the year traveling the length and breadth of the United States, speaking to various parent and professional groups. In schools, public and private, I seek out teachers who have taught for thirty years or more. I ask them, "How, in general, would you compare the typical child of today with the typical child you encountered during the early years of your teaching career?"

Without exception, these veteran teachers, having seen two generations of children parade through their classrooms, tell me that today's child is self-absorbed, lacking in respect, generally unwilling to accept responsibility, and inclined to give up quickly when a challenge turns the least bit frustrating. In other words, they describe today's child as deficient in the "Three R's" of

Respect, Responsibility, and Resourcefulness. This is hardly surprising. In fact, it is nothing more than the logical outcome of our break with the "Three R's" paradigm.

My mission, as I feel it, is to bring to American parents a clear vision of that "old-fashioned" paradigm; to persuade American parents that, despite the propagandizing of today's professional community, the philosophy of child rearing that guided our parents and their parents and their parents and so on is still valid. I am convinced, in fact, that if our culture is to survive the disintegrative forces that now threaten us, we must—regardless of skin color (keeping in mind that, skin color aside, we are all of one race), ethnicity, or religious beliefs—we must re-embrace with the "Three R's" in the rearing of our children.

"But I was raised by parents who believe in your 'Three R's,' " complained a woman in Sacramento, "and my self-esteem was all but destroyed by the time I reached adulthood."

Fact: In every generation, in every culture, regardless of the child-rearing paradigm that guides the culture, there will be a certain number of "bad" parents. That is inevitable. If you were reared by parents whom you consider, for whatever reason, "bad," it's important that you not confuse your parents' parenting practices with the child-rearing paradigm that prevailed in that era. The fact that your parents' *practices* were faulty does not mean the *paradigm* itself was faulty. You must separate the two and realize you can improve upon their practice while retaining the paradigm. Don't make the mistake of tossing the baby out with the bathwater.

Final Word: There is no inconsistency whatsoever between a valid definition of self-esteem and my "Three R's." A child raised to be respectful, responsible, and resourceful is a child fully equipped with the tools needed to successfully seek and discover self-esteem; or, as I prefer to call it, *self-competence.*

What about Fathers?

What about 'em? I've been a father for twenty-four years, so I know a few things about fatherhood. I know, for instance, that fathers are just as important as mothers to the rearing of children. I also know fathers don't get enough credit.

Beliefs aside, the average American still acts as if child rearing is primarily "women's work." As a result, there is a general tendency to ignore or minimize the contribution fathers can bring to the child-rearing process. The result of this lopsided state of affairs is that mothers tend to feel more responsible for their children than they actually are, while fathers often feel insignificant and even excluded. Worse yet, some fathers use this myth as an excuse to exclude themselves. In effect, many American mothers, even though married and living with their spouses, function as single parents.

To be sure, there are predictable differences in the ways mothers and fathers relate to and interact with their children. These differences have to do with biology, psychology, cultural expectations, and practical considerations. For example, in all cultures and in all times, mothers have occupied the role of primary parent during infancy and early childhood. This arrangement makes sense from several perspectives, including the fact that women have the built-in capability to feed their babies, while fathers do not.

But primary need not, should not, mean exclusive. Even during the early years, fathers are extremely important. Studies have shown, for example, that preschoolers whose fathers are actively involved in their upbringing tend to be more outgoing, adaptable, and accepting of challenge. Other research indicates that children with involved fathers do better in school, get along better with peers, and are more self-reliant. Children with active fathers are also less likely, during their teen years, to get pregnant or develop problems with alcohol and/or other drugs.

In *Never Cry Wolf,* his book that later became a Disney film, naturalist/author Farley Mowat gives us an insightful look at the wolf family, one of the few monogamous family units in the animal kingdom. Wolf cubs are never far from their mother. She protects and nurtures them until they reach adolescence, at which point the wolf father takes over as primary parent. He teaches his offspring to hunt and otherwise survive in an often hostile environment. In other words, while the wolf mother nurtures her young and endows them with trust, the wolf father endows them with the practical skills they will need for self-sufficiency.

Reading Mowat's book, the thought struck me that perhaps we humans would do well to take a lesson from the wolf. I am convinced, in fact, that children need more "mothering" than "fathering" during infancy and early childhood (but do not confuse *more* with exclusivity). I am equally convinced that as children grow and their needs for autonomy increase, fathers become increasingly important.

I can already hear the outcry: "Rosemond's a chauvinist! He's saying that, by themselves, women aren't capable of raising successful children!"

No, I'm not a chauvinist, and that's not what I'm saying. I'm a realist, and I'm saying that women are inherently better suited to certain aspects of parenting than fathers and *vice versa.* I'm saying that their respective strengths are better suited to certain areas and times of a child's development than others. I'm saying mothers and fathers contribute differently, but equally, to their children's "wholeness." I'm saying children fare better with two parents working together than with one of either gender working alone.

I'm not saying that all fathers would be wonderful dads if only given the chance. It's a father's responsibility to create opportunities for relationship with his children. If he doesn't, it sure as shootin' isn't their momma's fault.

Questions?

Q *We now realize we failed to accomplish certain goals with our daughter during her "twos." Namely, we perpetuated the myth that she was the single most important person in the family. As a result, she is clearly in charge at age four. Is it too late?*

A No, it isn't too late. It is more difficult, and more stressful on all concerned, to paddle back upstream, but it's not impossible. Furthermore, it is absolutely necessary that you do so, and the longer you wait, the more difficult and stressful it's going to be. Here's how:
• Begin paying more attention to one another than you pay to your daughter. Be husband and wife first, mother and father second. Stop including your daughter in everything you do. Let her know that the marriage is not a "threesome."

• Reread the section in this chapter on "The Benevolent Dictatorship." Establish the three understandings referred to therein.

• Assign your daughter a daily routine of chores around the home. In addition to picking up her things and keeping her room neat and clean, you can reasonably expect her to do such things as set and clear the table, help you load the dishwasher, mop hardwood and linoleum floors, dust furniture, and even run the vacuum in open areas of the home. Post the routine on the refrigerator, representing each chore with a picture. Putting her in a responsible, contributing position in the household is essential if she is to begin divesting herself of self-centeredness.

• Stop indulging her every whim. Learn to say "no," and learn to stand firm in the face of her protests. Remember that the more of a tolerance for frustration she develops, the more successfully self-reliant she will eventually become.

• Don't let her interrupt adult conversations, and don't let her include herself in adult gatherings. Likewise, keep a healthy distance from her recreation and peer relationships. In order for the marriage to have a life of its own, your daughter must have a life of her own as well.

Q My husband and I heard you speak in Hawaii and agreed with much of what you said. You lost me, however, with all the emphasis you put on not letting children be the center of attention in the family. After all, they're only children for a short time, and it seems to me that letting them be the center of attention for this relatively brief period in their lives does them no harm and helps the development of a positive self-image. So what's the big deal?

A The big deal is that no one, adult or child, ever gets something for nothing.

While children certainly enjoy being the center of their parents' attention, this seemingly "harmless" state of indulgence eventually impedes their happiness as adults. Letting children be the center of attention in a family extends their emotional dependency, making it nearly impossible for them ever to completely emancipate themselves. The center is too cozy, too warm and fuzzy. Who wants to leave?

Letting children be the center of attention in a family fails to teach them that happiness is something you make for yourself, not something someone else makes for you. A child with parents who try to keep him happy for eighteen years isn't likely to know how to keep himself happy from age eighteen on.

Letting children be the center of attention in a family prolongs their self-centeredness indefinitely, and nothing is quite as unattractive in an adult (or a child, for that matter) as self-centeredness. Furthermore, the self-centered adult can never be self-fulfilled because he's always looking for someone else to fulfill him.

Letting children be the center of attention in a family teaches them that self-worth is a function of how much attention they receive from other people. These children become attention addicts—forever unable to satisfy their need to be in the spotlight.

Letting children be the center of attention in a family turns the family upside down. The center of a family, for the sake of all concerned, should be strong and stable, a place people can rely upon. The only people potentially powerful enough to occupy that position of responsibility are adults. The child-centered family is, therefore, an insecure family consisting of insecure people who are trying hard not to let it show.

Letting children be the center of attention in a family increases the chances of disobedience. If you act as if your primary job is that of paying attention to your children, don't be surprised when they don't pay attention to you.

Letting children be the center of attention in a family puts on their small shoulders the responsibility of feeling that everything that goes wrong in the family, and especially conflict between their parents (which is inevitable), is their fault. The flip side of feeling like you're the most important person person in your family is the feeling you're the most influential as well. Guilt is the bogeyman that lurks in the background of the child-centered family.

Letting children be the center of attention in a family does absolutely nothing for their self-esteem. Self-esteem is something worked for, not given. It's developed in the course of

learning to stand on your own two feet, not while being allowed to stand on someone else's.
Is all that big deal enough?

Q *You've said children don't need a lot of attention, that too much is addicting, and that families should be adult-centered. How much attention is too much?*

A There is no way of quantifying the difference between giving a necessary amount of attention and giving too much. Suffice it to say the amount of attention a child needs is high during infancy and early toddlerhood and diminishes significantly and steadily thereafter. Dr. Burton White, America's most respected authority on early development and author of *The First Three Years of Life*, has said the single most significant sign of healthy development in a three-year-old is the child's ability to be self-occupied, without making unnecessary requests for adult attention, for relatively long periods of time (an hour or more). A three-year-old who has received too much adult attention will continue to demand high levels of it. On the other hand, a three-year-old who has not received enough will probably be depressed. Between these two extremes is a three-year-old who has received enough to ever-so-slightly more than enough attention and has learned to trust his parents without depending excessively upon them.

The tendency among middle- and upper-middle-class parents in our culture is to give children too much attention. This "sticks" a child at the center of the family, and results in a child who is demanding, disrespectful, and unappreciative.

To paraphrase Ecclesiastes, there's a time for giving attention and a time for expecting it. If you give too much, you'll get too little in return.

Q *My first child, a boy, is fifteen months old. I want to do everything I can to make our relationship a special one from the beginning. Specifically, I'd like to be not only a parent, but a true friend. What advice can you give me on accomplishing this?*

A I'd advise you not even to try, because it can't be done. The attempt, however, will cause more problems than you can now imagine. In the course of raising a child, there's a time for being a parent and a time—a much later time—for being a friend. You can't put the cart before the horse, nor can you put it alongside the horse. In this case, the horse is your authority and the cart is the potential for friendship contained within the relationship. This potential will become manifest, however, only if you exercise proper authority when it is due, and do not confuse the relationship with an attempt to occupy two roles at once.

In trying to be both friend and parent, you will fail at both. When the exercise of authority causes your child to become unhappy with you, as it often will, you will worry that you are destroying the friendship. As a consequence, you will be unable to take and maintain a firm stance on any issue. As your child learns to take advantage of your attempts to be a friend, your frustration will drive behavior that is decidedly unfriendly. This will not only introduce conflict and confusion into the relationship, but will also saddle you with an almost constant burden of guilt. Under the circumstances, your child is likely to grow up either resenting you or manipulating you, neither of which forms the basis for an eventual friendship.

In short, the better a true parent you are during the first eighteen years or so of your child's life, the better friends you will later be. Put first things first.

Q *My thirty-three-month-old daughter insists that I do everything for her. She screams if her father picks her up. She runs away from him if he approaches her or tries to help her with something. She refuses to kiss him, won't let him tuck her in, help with her clothes, or even get her a drink of water. If he looks at her, she says, "Tell Daddy to stop looking at me!" This started about a month ago, and it's gotten progressively worse since. What have we done wrong? What should we do?*

A The difficulty you're having with your daughter is not as uncommon as you may think. The cases I've seen of "father-rejection syndrome"—and there have been many—have all shared a fairly uniform set of characteristics:

- The problem began when the child was two years old, give or take a few months.
- The parent of preference is always the mother.
- Mom is usually a homemaker.
- The child is usually female.
- The child is usually the couple's first.

Almost all children exhibit a slight, but clear preference for one parent (usually mother) over the other until well into the third year of life. There are two periods during infancy and toddlerhood when this attachment is especially strong. The first occurs between eight and twelve months, the other between eighteen and twenty-four months. The latter is usually the more problematic. An eighteen-month-old is verbal, mobile, and considerably more demanding and persistent than an eight-month-old. The picture is further complicated by the fact that at the same time parents begin establishing their authority, the child is learning to assert her will upon the family. Children this age seem to possess an intuitive genius for seizing control of issues germaine to the question, "Who runs the show around here?"

That's exactly what your daughter has done. Your problems are over if you stop believing that she will not let her father do anything for her. As long as you believe she is competent to make this decision, she will believe it too, and she will refuse to have it any other way. On the other hand, when you decide to lift the burden of this responsibility from her small shoulders, she will, after screaming and carrying on for a while, make the necessary adjustment and life will go on.

Find a quiet time to say something along these lines: "Daughter dear, from now on Mommy is not going to do everything for you. Daddy is going to help you, too. He is going to get you water and put on your coat and help with your bath . . . (and so on). If you want to scream when Daddy helps you, that's okay. You can scream and you can roll on the floor and kick and drool, but Daddy is going to help you anyway."

Don't make the talk too long-winded, and don't act as if you're seeking her permission to make this administrative policy change. The purpose is not to win her approval or a guarantee of cooperation, but simply to give her fair warning that things are going to be different.

From then on, if she wants water, the parent in the better position should get the water. If Dad gets it and she refuses to drink it, that's her problem. Dad should leave the glass of water where she can reach it and walk away. If someone has to help her on with her coat, and Dad is the more convenient someone to do that, then Dad should do it. If she struggles and screams, Dad should do it anyway (firmly but gently), and Mom must not come to the rescue.

Where kisses are concerned, Daddy should definitely not force his affections upon his daughter, but if he's carrying her and it feels natural for him to kiss her, then he should feel no reservations about kissing her. He might even turn this into a game of "Steal-a-Kiss." A little humor always helps defuse situations of this sort.

It may take some time, but your daughter will get used to it. That's a promise.

Q *You've said that three-year-olds who demand lots of attention have probably received too much to begin with. You were talking about my thirty-four-month-old son. As a result of my excessive "mommying," he follows me around the house all day, wanting me to play with him, read to him, get him this, do that. As soon as I begin to do something for myself, he interrupts. I feel like I have no time to myself, no life outside that of being Ryan's mother. How can I undo this?*

A First of all, you are not guilty as charged. Women have been encouraged to buy into the falsehood that the more attention they pay their children, the better mothers they are. Female parents in our culture do not have full permission to have lives of their own, to pursue personal or professional goals, much less say "no" to their kids and mean it.

You're not guilty. You've just fallen into what I call the "Mommy Trap." In the process of paying so much unnecessary attention to Ryan, you've neglected yourself. If you want to help Ryan become more independent, you must begin controlling his access to you. You must let him know, in no uncertain terms, that you are not at his beck and call.

If you can stand some unhappiness (temporary, I assure you) on his part, here are some tried and proven suggestions:

• Make it easier for Ryan to do certain things on his own. If, for example, he frequently asks you for a cup of juice, put a small easy-pour container of juice on a low table every morning and teach him to pour his own.

• Pick three things Ryan frequently wants you to do for him, but which he can do for himself. Cut pictures out of magazines to represent each demand and glue them on a piece of construction paper onto which you also glue a picture of Ryan. When finished, you have a poster that says, in effect, "Ryan can, and will, do these things on his own." Put the poster on the refrigerator, telling him what it means. Tell him you can't—not *won't*, but *can't*—do the things represented for him anymore because he's a "big boy." From then on, when Ryan asks you for one of the things on the poster, take him over to it and say, "This means you can do that for yourself. I can't do it for you anymore, remember?"

• Set aside thirty minutes every morning and every afternoon for Ryan. When you have the time to play with him or read to him, announce that it's now "Mommy Time!" Set your stove timer to ring in thirty minutes. Tell him that when the bell rings, it means you have to stop and go back to your own work (or reading, or whatever).

Ryan will, no doubt, be initially unhappy with these limits. But if you're firm and consistent, he'll make a relatively quick adjustment.

Chapter 2

Promoting Healthy Development

Your little one's first eight months of life were a time of almost complete dependency. As he acquired the ability to move about the environment under his own power, gains in cognitive (problem-solving), physical/motor, and communication skills began accelerating. In the process, he came gradually to the realization he didn't need you to be his "gofer"; rather, he could do things for himself, on his own, thank you. And, to paraphrase the country song, that's when your heartaches (or headaches, or both) began.

Swiss developmental psychologist Jean Piaget dubbed the first eighteen months of life the *sensori-motor period*. By that he meant children at this stage are insatiable collectors of information. They are constantly on the move, harvesting and cataloging sensory data regarding the environment. Their explorations are random but comprehensive. This age child has no blueprint, just an irresistible urge to know everything there is to know about every "thing" there is.

Throughout his meanderings, the toddler absorbs an incredible amount of information without, however, knowing how to *use* it. Then, sometime around his eighteenth month, he realizes he can act upon the world to *make things happen*. His guidance systems suddenly switch from automatic to autonomous pilot. Before, he was an explorer, Christopher Columbus reincarnate, out to discover the "New World." Now, however, he becomes an experimenter, a little scientist, intent upon finding out how things work.

As the "sense" of the environment is revealed, the toddler begins interacting with it not just curiously, but purposefully, to *solve problems.* This quantum leap heralds the advent of what Piaget termed the *pre-operational period,* during which the child begins to acquire, by trial-and-error, the ability to think in terms of cause-and-effect and, therefore, *operate* meaningfully on the environment.

Contrast: A fifteen-month-old, seeing a jar of cookies on the kitchen counter, will reach in vain, fall on his butt, and scream bloody murder until someone comes along to lend a helpful hand. Several months later, that same child, spying the same jar of cookies, will push a chair to the counter, climb up, and get the cookies for himself.

As the child's mind expands, so does the world. In no time he is consumed with excitement, a virtual factory of activity. He is "on the go" during every waking moment, "getting into everything," climbing on counters and bookshelves, climbing out of his crib and car seat, always one step ahead of his parents. One thing's for certain: he won't take "no" for an answer. And why should he, when everything around and inside him is saying "Yes! Yes! Yes!" (except his parents, who are constantly repeating "No! No! No!")?

One of the limitations nature has imposed on two-year-olds is a gap between physical and intellectual development, favoring the latter. In other words, their physical skills have yet to catch up with their mental ones. A two-year-old may be able to visualize the solution to a problem, but unable to perform the movements required to carry it out. For example, it may be perfectly clear to him that a certain shape fits a certain space in a puzzle. Nonetheless, he cannot make his fingers work well enough to maneuver it into place. This frustrating disparity is often expressed in sudden and sometimes destructive tantrums. If someone tries to lend a helpful hand, the child may become all the more enraged. His frustration aside, he would still rather do it himself and fail than watch you succeed. Can you blame him?

Sometime around the middle of his second year, the child realizes, in one relatively sudden, insightful moment, that he's a "Me." This is the flowering of individuality, of self-consciousness. For the next eighteen months or so, the child goes about the task of defining who "Me" is and establishing clear title to that psychological territory. Much to his dismay, as we've already established in chapter 1, he must accept that his boundaries (therefore, his influence) are not all-encompassing. "Me" is not the biggest fish in the sea, but one of many. He must learn that independence does not mean doing as he pleases. Just as it is the child's task at this age to establish autonomy (a clear sense of separateness, of individual identity), his parents' task is that of commencing the socialization process. This requires setting realistic expectations as well as communicating and enforcing appropriate limits. As his physical and mental aptitudes expand, and (correspondingly) his desire to master the environment enlarges, so his parents begin making more and more demands upon him. They tell him he must do this, and he mustn't do that; he can't touch this, and he can't have that.

It gradually dawns on him that he can't possess the proverbial cake and eat it too. He cannot, in other words, be independent and comfortably dependent at the same time. In order to become autonomous, he must give up a like measure of attachment to his parents, and Mommy in particular. Whether it is more advantageous to be independent or dependent is a difficult issue to resolve. As a result, the young toddler is a study in contrast: clinging and cuddly one minute, demanding and defiant the next. He wants the best of both worlds. Don't we all?

As the preceding discussion suggests, the behaviors associated with the so-called "terrible" twos can be explained in terms of either developmental events, such as gaining the ability to climb, or psychosocial ones, as in parents' attempts to socialize. It is important, therefore, to understand that these behaviors—getting into everything, tantrums, refusing to cooperate, and so on—are *normal*. Unfortunately, many parents seem to regard them as abberations that require harsh punishment. True, limits must be set on the child, but there are ways of doing this that do not compromise the child's ability to expand his understanding of how the world works. True, the child must learn that his parents are running the show, but this can be accomplished without suppressing the child's sense of self. True, the child must learn he can't always get what he wants (my thanks to Mick Jagger of the Rolling Stones for this insight), when he wants it, but this can be done without damage to the child's strong-willed spirit. (Oh, by the way, concerning the bad press the *strong-willed* child has been getting in recent years from various parenting experts, I'd like to meet the parent who would pray for a *weak-willed* child. We should all join together in blessing strong-willed children, for they are surely the future movers and shakers of the planet.)

Before we go any further, let's take a moment to paint a word picture of two-year-olds in terms of the developmental and psychosocial influences that characterize the age:

• Two-year-olds are consumed with the desire to figure everything out. Therefore, they are highly active and "get into everything."

• They have yet to develop a tolerance for frustration. Therefore, when things do not go their way—when people do not successfully read their minds, when they don't get what they want when they want it, when their fingers will not cooperate with their eyes and minds—they suffer instantaneous cerebral meltdown accompanied by much wailing and thrashing about.

• We are talking about children who are only slightly socialized. Therefore, when they explode, they do so with no regard for where they are or who might be watching.

• Two-year-olds still believe they control their parents. They're also developing a clearer sense of themselves as autonomous persons. Therefore, they steadfastly refuse to cooperate with their parents' instructions.

• Twos have every reason to believe that their parents exist to pay attention to them; therefore, they pay infuriatingly little attention to their parents. So, they run away from their parents in stores, and they ignore their parents' instructions, and other equally oblivious things.

• Verbal and intellectual skills are growing by leaps and bounds. Therefore, two-year-olds ask lots of questions. They are self-centered, so they talk to themselves a lot, and when they talk to other people, they're often in their own little world. What results is a monologue that makes little sense. If you are the audience to one of these soliloquies, don't worry about understanding what's being said (because you won't) or making any sense yourself. Just nod your head, look interested, and say whatever comes to mind (as in a word association exercise). These "conversations" have no rules and can be fun.

• As the mind expands, so does the imagination. Older twos,

therefore, invent both imaginary friends and fears of many sorts.

• Twos tend to want everything on their terms. When you want to pick them up and give them a cuddle, they push away. When both of your hands are busy with something else, they demand to be picked up and cuddled.

• Their egocentricity knows no bounds; therefore, they think you should be able to read their minds. They want milk. You bring milk. They scream and knock the milk off the table. You fool! They said milk, but meant orange juice. You apologize and bring orange juice. They knock it off the table. Wrong cup! You bring orange juice in the right cup, meanwhile, they've decided milk doesn't sound so bad after all, so . . . and on and on it goes. The good news is they tend to sleep anywhere from twelve to fourteen hours a day. The bad news is some of them hardly sleep at all.

In short, this is the best of times, but it can also be the worst of times. And that pretty well sums it up, eh?

Milestones

Preferring broader strokes, I do not intend to dwell on the details of your child's development. If your curiosity is piqued by the upcoming summation (and I hope it is), I encourage you to broaden your education by reading *The First Three Years of Life* by developmental psychologist Burton White, who has carried out the most comprehensive of such developmental investigations to date.

I will simply point out that human children develop along four dimensions, which we artificially separate for purposes of discussion. They are: social/emotional, physical/motor, cognitive (intellectual), and verbal (linguistic). In reality, each dimension, each developmental "system," is inseparable from the other three. If, for example, you impede a toddler's physical/motor development by, say, confining him to a playpen for significant periods of time, you will also impair the development of verbal, social/emotional, and cognitive skills. Likewise, a child whose cognitive growth is relatively slow is also likely to exhibit delays in social/emotional, verbal, and physical/motor development.

Understanding that these four developmental areas are four components of a larger, unified whole, we will now look at each area as if it were separate. For the sake of simplicity and brevity, I've chosen a chart format (see figures 2-1 through 2-4). Keep in mind that age designations are but rough approximations of when, in most cases, certain milestones are reached. If, for example, your child is twenty-eight months old and falls on his butt every time he tries to kick a stationary ball or falls on his face every time he tries to run, don't panic. That most children have acquired these skills by twenty-four months is no cause for alarm. More often than not, skills in one area will surge temporarily ahead, somewhat at the expense of gains in the other three. It's as if the child has a finite amount of "developmental energy" at his disposal. If, during a certain period of his toddlerhood, he "assigns" the majority of this energy to the cognitive realm, then we'll see lots of progress taking place in problem-solving. At the same time, relatively little may be taking place along verbal, physical/motor, or emotional/social lines. Have patience. At this age, as long as things are up to par in at least one area, slight delays (the operative word being *slight*) in the other three are nothing to fret over. The developmentally "at risk" toddler is generally lagging in all four areas simultaneously.

There is something to be said for not knowing when the "normal" child passes certain milestones because few children pass them all "normally." If, therefore, you don't want your anxiety level raised, don't look at the charts. If you can't contain your curiosity, look at the charts, but please take them with a grain of sodium chloride. Regardless, if you have concerns, you should, by all means, check them out with your pediatrician or family physician. (Here it should be noted that pediatricians and family physicians tend to become somewhat annoyed when parents do not consult them before making appointments with psychologists or other child specialists. As a psychologist, I couldn't agree with them more. Please, please do yourself, your child, and your pocketbook a big favor by running any and all developmental and behavioral concerns by your child's physician. If the doc feels there may be a problem, he will refer you to the person he feels is, first, most qualified to provide the service, and second, most likely to communicate and work cooperatively with him concerning your child's developmental and behavioral needs.)

Physical/Motor Development (figure 2–1)

by 18 months: stacks two fist-size blocks
scribbles when given a crayon
throws things (with pushing motion)
grasps small objects with thumb and forefinger
crawls up and down stairs
walks unassisted
uses spoon to feed self (but still messy)

by 24 months: kicks stationary ball
runs (albeit awkwardly, often tripping)
pushes or pulls toy while walking
beginning to climb
can open some doors, operate some latches

by 30 months: beginning to favor one hand over the other
stacks six blocks
climbs in and out of adult chair unassisted
in general, climbing is becoming more "daring"
jumps with both feet off ground
walks up and down stairs unassisted
alternates feet when walking up stairs
tries to ride tricycle (give this one some time)
feeds self without much messiness (but still a lot
of spills)

by 36 months: consistently favors one hand over the other
stacks eight blocks
beginning to throw ball overhand
performs simple two-handed tasks
assembles simple wooden puzzle (after
demonstration)
holds book and turns pages
has started using fork

Cognitive (Intellectual) Development (figure 2-2)

by 18 months: takes (or attempts to take) things apart
learns new skills and behaviors through
imitation
moves obstacle aside to retrieve something else
utilizes repetition (e.g., flipping on and off a
light switch) to learn cause and effect
almost constant exploratory behavior
begins using trial-and-error to solve problems

by 24 months: begins anticipating consequences of own behavior—and certain events
climbs on chair to retrieve something
uses functional toys appropriately (throws ball,
cuddles doll, pulls toy train)
curiosity shifts from objects to events and
human interactions
spends more and more time looking out
windows
insightful problem-solving emerges (thinks
things through, often described as "clever")
less impulsive, more generally thoughtful (one
can "see the wheels turning")
first purposeful creations (mostly scribbles)

by 30 months: can put simple puzzles together with guidance
noticeably excellent memory for places, people
first truly representational drawings
play is generally more organized, purposeful
denies doing something in order to escape consequences (note: this is *not* lying)
thinks anything that moves is alive (blown
leaves, flowing water, flushing toilet)

> begins making associations (e.g., umbrellas are
> for when it rains)
> gets excited when one thing reminds of another

by 36 months: is learning to wait for requests to be met
shows understanding of size relationships by
stacking smaller blocks on larger ones
shows understanding of spatial relationships by
using three blocks to build a "bridge"
masters simple wooden puzzle after
demonstration
plans and carries out complicated activities
can generalize (keys open doors)
cannot grasp abstract moral concepts (good,
truth)
begins to understand concepts of quantity
(more, bigger), but still has difficulty with
qualitative comparisons (better, prettier)

Social/Emotional Development (figure 2-3)

by 18 months: prefers drinking from cup
expresses wants without crying
hugs and kisses familiar people
takes own clothes off
demonstrates understanding of routines
abrupt emotional changes

by 24 months: wants to be center of attention
increased reluctance to separate from parents
plays alongside, but not with, other children
displays fairly complete range of emotions
helps with simple household tasks (picking up
toys)

throws tantrums when frustrated
defiant demonstrations of independence
("No!")
runs ahead of caregiver

by 30 months: possessive of toys and parents
showing interest in toilet
resists change of routine
tantrums and defiance reaching a peak
resists help in solving problems
once again separates more easily from caregiver
seeks praise for accomplishments
demanding
plays in groups, but not cooperatively
emotional changes are less abrupt
attempts to put on own clothes (and occasionally
succeeds)

by 36 months: increasing emotional stability (fewer "swings")
puts on underpants, maybe a T-shirt (backward)
uses toilet consistently (still can't wipe self)
invents imaginary friends
inexplicable fears develop (the dark, a certain
room)
plays interactively, perhaps cooperatively,
in group
takes turns (if supervised and directed by adult)
begins to play one-on-one with other children
shares spontaneously on occasion
shows affection toward other children and
adults
pretend play begins to dominate
directs adults in pretend play

Verbal (Linguistic) Development (figure 2-4)

by 18 months: imitates words
uses one-word sentences ("Milk!")
uses inflections, emphasis
can correctly point to at least one body part
can correctly point out objects in familiar
picture
enjoys looking at pictures in books, magazines
follows simple directions
enjoys being read to, sits through short story
twenty-word vocabulary

by 24 months: refers to self as "me" or by own name
uses two-word sentences ("Me go!")
imitates phrases, but omits prepositions and
articles
one-hundred-word vocabulary
correctly points to objects in unfamiliar picture
follows two-step directions
begins carrying out more complex directions
gives own name when asked
points correctly to parts of face, basic body parts

by 30 months: begins using three- or four-word sentences
begins using prepositions ("Turn on water.")
uses plural form of some words
becomes frustrated when not understood
names objects in a picture when asked "what's
this?"
asks "what's this?" often incessantly
begins "conversing" with others, but often talks
as if "off in own world"

by 36 months: describes objects according to function
uses longer, complete sentences
may, at times, talk constantly
talks loudly and insistently to get attention
asks more complex questions ("When?" "How?")
carries out more complex directions
uses present and past tense of verbs
begins using possessive form ("Daddy's car")

Facilitating Your Child's Development

Barring genetic problems of one sort or another, every human being is, from the moment of conception, programmed for competency. In order to activate this tremendously rich and varied program, all parents need to do is *provide the growing child with stimulating environments and a variety of interesting experiences that together serve to enable the exercise of competency behaviors.* This is nothing more than a developmental formula for bringing out the best in a child, and every adult who lives with, teaches, or takes care of children shares that pressing moral responsibility.

Seeing to this obligation is neither difficult nor technologically demanding, and there is great benefit to both parent and child in doing so. If you properly assist the development of competency skills, your child will become more independent more quickly, and as you probably already know, his ability to occupy his own time creatively will be the greatest of all boons to you. So, wasting no time, here are some dos and don'ts for setting up a home-based competency program. Most of it can be accomplished for next to nothing.

Child-proof your home: Put well out of reach anything that poses a health hazard to your youngster (cleaning fluids, bottles of alcohol-based products, knives, medicines, etc.) as well as items that are valuable and/or irreplaceable (heirloom ceramics, crystal, old photographs, etc.). Child-proof as much of the house as possible in order to "open" it to your child's explorations. Don't, however, just make your home safe; make it stimulating as well. Put things within your child's reach that will be interesting for him to handle and taste and take apart. The more opportunities a child has to express curiosity, the more his mind will expand. See chapter 3, "Creative Discipline," for an expanded discussion of child-proofing.

Minimize the use of playpens and other restrictive furniture and devices: This injunction also applies to cribs, walkers, high chairs, and table seats. Playpens have their pros and cons. Used wisely and sparingly, a playpen can perform a valuable service for parents as well as provide a toddler with a safe, albeit temporary (please!), place to stay while a parent cooks, talks on the phone, or goes to the bathroom. Keep in mind, however, that "playpen" is a misnomer, because children do not play in them, not for long, anyway. Overused, a playpen can be an obstacle to normal development. When left unattended in playpens for long periods, children become bored, frustrated, and even depressed. The best policy is not to use a playpen for more than a few minutes at a time, no more than three or four times a day. If possible, put the playpen in the room you'll be in and talk to your child while you go about your business.

Encourage and promote a variety of outdoor activities: Make sure your child enjoys plenty of outdoor time. Toddlers generally love to play in sand, be pushed in a swing, take walks, or just roam out of doors, collecting things. While your child is outside, it's perfectly acceptable for you to do nothing but sit and just watch or read a book as long as you balance these sorts of things with some playful interaction. Remember, whether pushing your tot on a swing, rolling a ball back and forth between you, or wrestling in the grass, it's never too late to have a happy childhood!

Encourage and promote indoor activity: The more time your child spends indoors, the more important it is that you provide opportunities for large-muscle development. If you don't provide a menu of appropriate activities, your naturally active and curious child will no doubt invent some that won't be to your liking (e.g., scaling bookshelves). Indoor slides, indoor climbing apparatuses, and other equipment of this sort stimulate gross-motor development. Since young children love nothing more than bouncing on their beds, you might even consider buying a sturdy box spring, setting it off to one side of your child's room or playroom, and letting him bounce on it to his heart's content.

Encourage and promote fine-motor development: It's as important that children develop good fine-motor skills as it is that they develop good gross-motor ones. Provide your toddler with plenty of crayons and paper, blocks, and interlocking construction toys such as those from Lego (the toddler line is called Duplo). Show your child how things work, how they come apart, and how to put them back together.

Read to your child: A home-based competency program recognizes not only the growing child's need for physical activity, but also his need for intellectual and creative stimulation. Being read to fits the bill perfectly. Beginning no later than age six months, preschoolers should be read to each and every day. Initially, because your child's attention span is short, these sessions will last no longer than five minutes or so. By age three, you should be reading to your child no less than thirty minutes a day.

Talk to your child: Converse, even if the child's "conversation" makes little, if any, sense. Demonstrate and talk about how things work. Ask simple questions and answer your child's questions with simple, direct answers. Before going into a store or any other public situation, tell your child how you expect him to behave. Use language your child can understand; language that's concrete as opposed to being filled with lots of grown-up abstractions (e.g., "good").

Don't buy your child lots of toys: Too many toys smother a child's ability to make choices and be creative. You can help develop your child's imagination and resourcefulness (the ability to do a lot with a little) by not buying him a lot. Where toys are concerned, less is definitely more. The few toys you buy should be ones your child can take apart on his own and that allow for lots of creative, constructive behavior. Crayons, clay, Lincoln Logs, Lego (or Duplo), Bristle Blocks, and large cardboard "bricks" are appropriate.

When parents ask, "How can we know a worthwhile toy from one that's a waste of money?" I answer, "If a toy was in production before 1955, it's probably fine." With few exceptions, every toy manufactured since then has been nothing more than an attempt to reinvent an already-existing wheel. Remember also that in most cases a toddler would rather play with the box a toy came in than the toy itself. When our son, Eric, was two, his toys consisted of some large cardboard bricks, a toy truck, a couple of stuffed animals, a ball, and a large appliance box I'd made into a playhouse. He could play for hours by himself, proving it's not important how many toys a child has, but what he's able to do with them. So-called "educational" toys? Children can do without them. Generally speaking, claims that a certain toy was designed to promote such-and-such a specific developmental skill are hollow. Essential developmental skills will emerge on their own as long as a child is allowed sufficient opportunity to explore and experiment with a variety of everyday things.

Shut off the television: Watching television is a "passivity," not an "activity." Not only is the watcher physically inactive, he's mentally inactive as well. According to reliable figures, verified by Nielsen survey after Nielsen survey, the average American preschool child watches an amazing five thousand hours of television before age six (and Nielsen doesn't even count hours watched before a child's second birthday)! That's one-fourth of a child's discretionary time; time that otherwise would be spent in meaningful physical and mental activity of the kind that promotes creativity, imagination, and intelligence. Remember our formula for promoting competency behaviors? Consider that television is not an experience that involves the excercise of any competency skill. It therefore lends nothing of value to the life of a growing child. In fact, developmentally speaking, television is a *deprivational experience*, which is why I recommend not exposing a child to much, if any, television until he or she has learned to read and reads well. (More on this topic later in this chapter.)

Play with your child: While I'm by no means suggesting that you should become your child's primary playmate, it's important that you make time for relaxed, playful interactions with your toddler. Play is, after all, the most important thing young children do. Play promotes the growth of imagination and creativity. Games of "let's pretend," which children begin showing interest in shortly after their second birthdays, help them understand and prepare for adult roles. More sophisticated games, which come later, promote social problem-solving skills and help children develop healthy attitudes toward competition. Play also provides children a safe way of expressing socially unacceptable thoughts and feelings. The list goes on: Play exercises gross- and fine-motor skills, strengthens language development, and stretches attention span. In addition, play bolsters initiative and resourcefulness. Because it is self-rewarding, play fosters good self-esteem. Last, but by no means least, because it is fun, play helps children develop a good sense of humor.

Studies show that children who enjoy ample opportunity for play are more independent, resourceful, and tolerant of frustration. When they go to school, they are, by and large, the better readers. They are more curious and imaginative. They have better social skills, are less aggressive, and are better at both winning *and* losing. They like themselves better. All in all, they are more fun to be around, for both adults *and* other children.

Playing with a toddler is as simple as providing a few things to play with (a ball, some blocks, a few toy cars) and letting the child take the lead. Just let yourself be a kid again! Roll the ball back and forth, build a block tower and knock it down, crash your cars together! Laugh! Also, don't forget that too many toys and television both throw a wet blanket over the child's playful inclinations.

A True Tale of Too Many Toys

A couple consulted me concerning their almost-three-year-old daughter, Amanda: "Amanda doesn't want to let us out of her sight," they said. "She follows us around the house, constantly asks us to play with her, and whines if we can't. Neither of us minds playing with her some, but don't understand why—with all the toys she has—she can't entertain herself occasionally."

My ears perked up. "How many toys does she have?" I asked.

Amanda's dad spoke up. "She has so many you can't walk into her room without stepping on one. We go to the toy store at least twice a month, maybe more. I suppose we've been guilty of spoiling her."

That was the problem, in a nutshell. Not only did Amanda have too many toys, she had all the wrong kinds. First, the confusion of toys in her life made it all but impossible for her to figure out how to use her time. It presented her with too many choices. Second, the playthings themselves were one-dimensional toys that were of little "play value" (see the first question at the end of this chapter for an explanation of this concept). Instead of toys that could be many things, each of her toys was one thing, and one thing only. A toy car was forever a toy car and nothing more.

Paradoxically, Amanda's environment, while full of fancy things, failed to offer sufficient imaginative stimulation and opportunities for creative play. In short, Amanda was bored, and for good reason. The more toys she received, the more bored she became, and the more she looked toward her parents to unbore her.

The first thing I had Amanda's parents do was give about ninety percent of her toys to a children's charity. The remaining ten percent included soft, cuddly dolls (that neither walked nor talked nor wet their pants), small human and animal figures, blocks, and a dollhouse. I helped them rate Amanda's toys according to play value on a scale of one to ten, and they boxed those with ratings of less than eight.

Next, Amanda's parents went toy shopping. This time, however, they bought toys that would spark Amanda's imagination and, therefore, keep her interest. These included toys that were multidimensional, meaning toys that could be taken apart and put together again in a variety of different ways.

To create a household environment that encouraged exploration, Amanda's parents child-proofed their home. In addition to making for a safe, stimulating environment, child-proofing also meant that Amanda would hear the word "no" far less often. Power struggles would be minimized, making obedience more likely.

Amanda's parents put safety latches on all the kitchen cabinets but one, which became "Amanda's cabinet." They stocked this cubby hole with empty oatmeal boxes, empty spools, old pots and pans, small boxes of all sorts, and other safe household items that might otherwise have been discarded. Amanda could come here at any time and rummage to her heart's content.

Last, but not least, Amanda's parents obtained a large appliance box into which they cut a door and several windows. A small chair went inside, along with a pillow and a few dolls. Just the place for hours of imagination.

Within a couple of weeks of these changes, Amanda was playing on her own most of the day, making far fewer demands on her parents, and acting, in their words, "bright and happy again." Proving, once again, that less is more.

Two True Tales of Television

Every so often, I get up on my Television-Is-Bad-for-Kids soapbox and attempt the all but impossible: persuading parents that television really *does* rot the brains of children.

I don't mean that literally, of course, but I do mean that regardless of the program, "Sesame Street" included, it wastes their precious time. And their time is of the essence. Study after study confirms that children have about five or six years to get their acts together, so to speak; to get in touch with and develop the many talents and abilities that constitute nearly every human child's incredibly vast and rich genetic heritage.

It's all there from the moment of conception, waiting for a chance to strut its wondrous stuff. Artistic, athletic, intellectual, or musical talent—you name it, almost every kid's got it. And nothing more is required to release this magic than to provide children with *environments and experiences that enable the exercise of excellence.* Again, this is nothing more than a formula for bringing forth the best in a child: Put the child of potential in an environment that is both stimulating and receptive to exploration, one that provides experiences that exercise the child's God-given talents and abilities, add the energy and enthusiasm of childhood, and you've got the makings for excellence. That simple.

The key, of course, is the environment, which is where my tirade against television begins. In the last thirty years, television has become a primary environment for our nation's children. They spend more time watching than they spend doing anything else, even going to school. All this watching must be having a profound effect on their development, and it can't be good, because a child watching television is exercising not one— I repeat, *not one*—competency skill. And one look at his blank expression will tell you more than words could ever express that this isn't energy and this isn't enthusiasm. This isn't childhood! It's nothing! It's a waste of time; precious, irretrievable time!

I'd shout it from the rooftops if I thought the guys in white coats wouldn't come and take me away. Instead, I talk about it every opportunity I get, because I think each and every child has a right to become as complete and competent as he or she was meant to become.

Several years ago, I said all this to an audience at a church in Charlotte, North Carolina. Several weeks later, I received a letter from one of the parents who'd been in attendance. She wrote: "Although skeptical that you could convince me that watching 'Sesame Street' was harmful, I went with an open mind. I was always proud of my two daughters'—ages four and two—ability to sit and watch PBS programs by the hour. I thought that since they had never seen a commercial and only watched 'educational' programs, they would be unscathed. I returned home from your lecture and turned off the television. We haven't seen a program since. What amazes me is how we don't miss it at all, and also how much more time we have available to us. Toys that haven't been touched since last Christmas are now being played with daily. We read more stories together and enjoy our days more since we aren't following the television schedule. Thank you for changing our lives."

This mother's experience with turning off the television is hardly unique. A Waterloo, Iowa, mother and speech therapist, after hearing me speak on the subject, decided to see for herself whether my warnings about the effects of television-watching held any truth. Here, in her words, is her story:

"Because of your lecture, we established a no-television policy in our home when our daughter, Rachel, was twenty-five months old. Since then, the only television she's watched consists of videotapes chosen especially for family viewing. This amounts to one or two animated films per week. Furthermore, we only watch a movie after we've read the book together. We noticed an immediate improvement in Rachel's speech and language skills after the television blackout. At twenty-five months (still watching television), she was finally putting two words together. One month after silencing the television, she'd gone from two-word utterances to singing 'Angels Watching Over Me, Lord.' Three months later, she was retelling *Cinderella* and other favorite books and using as many as nine words per sentence. Before the blackout, she would sit motionless in front of the tube, eyes glued to the screen. She now engages in amazing amounts of make-believe—pretending to be Cinderella, dropping a slipper while she runs away from the 'prince' (our cat) and asking me to 'peeten' with her. I'm now thoroughly convinced of the merits of pulling the plug. Speaking as both a mother and professional, I don't believe Rachel would have developed her present skills if we had continued to allow her to watch television an average of two hours per day, as she had done before."

I've said it before, and I'll say it again: television-watching pacifies the growing child's intellect and imagination and interferes significantly with the development of social, perceptual, motor, and language/communication skills. This is true regardless of the program being watched and is why controversy over the content of certain so-called "children's programs" is nothing more than a red herring. The observation that children show significant developmental gains once television is drastically cut back in their lives, if not removed altogether, is universal. I invite you to prove it to yourselves.

On Reading to Your Child

"What can I do to help my child become a successful reader?" is one of the most frequent questions parents ask me. I begin by explaining that reading is not one skill, but the interplay of several:

Inquiry. Reading is, first and foremost, an act of inquiry, exploration, and discovery. Reading is one of the best ways a child can learn about the workings of the world around him. An inquisitive baby rummages through drawers and cabinets in search of knowledge. In the same way, and for the same reason, an inquisitive three-year-old rummages through the pages of a book.

Imagination. Reading is an act of imagination. A toddler transforms words into images in the same way he transforms a shoe box into a boat. Imagination is essential to comprehension. It breathes life into the static word, making it dynamic. Without imagination, words are hollow, devoid of meaning. The child who has misplaced her imagination (or had it displaced) will approach reading as a chore rather than a joy.

Coordination. Reading involves the coordination of physical and mental processes—hands, eyes, and brain. Hands hold the book, turning the pages and adjusting the depth of field such that the eyes can easily scan lines of print, transmitting raw data to the brain. The brain operates actively on that data, decoding, retrieving information stored in its vast data bank, making associations, forming mental images—all of which culminates in the "Ah-ha!" of comprehension.

Self-esteem. Saying that a child has "good self-esteem" is really a rather abstract way of saying the child enjoys being challenged. Reading, like every other challenge, offers a child the opportunity to grow intellectually, creatively, emotionally, and socially. The child with good self-esteem will welcome the opportunity.

A successful reader, therefore, is an inquisitive, imaginative, well-coordinated child with good self-esteem. Keeping that in mind, there are three things a parent can do to encourage the growth of reading skills.

• *Provide safe, stimulating environments that encourage the growth of inquiry and imagination.* If, from his earliest months, a child's inquiries into the world are rewarding (as opposed to frustrating), if his parents feed (as opposed to starve) his appetite for discovery, he will want, when the time comes, to rummage as eagerly through books as he did through drawers and cabinets when he was younger.

• *Spend lots of time reading to children.* There are few things more completely enriching to a child—emotionally, socially, and intellectually—than being read to. Nestled securely in his parents' arms, listening to them paint word-pictures, a child learns that reading feels good.

• *Read themselves.* Children follow the examples parents set. If parents read, a child will follow suit. If, on the other hand, parents rely on the television as their primary source of entertainment and information, a child will see no value in reading.

Spacing

"How far apart should we space our children?" is a question frequently asked by today's parents. As the size of the average American family has shrunk, concern over the issue of spacing has increased.

Dr. Burton White has found that, generally speaking, three and one-half years is the ideal interval between siblings. Contrary to what many parents think, the chance of problems with the older child and within the sibling relationship increases not only as that ideal interval shortens, but also as it lengthens. In other words, parents are just as likely to have problems with a spacing of five years as they are with one and one-half.

The problem with early spacing is that the first child may not yet be ready to do with less parental attention when the second child comes along. When this is the case, the older child's development may "stall" as he struggles to keep the baby from taking his place in the spotlight. By thirty-six months, most children have achieved a satisfactory degree of autonomy and are not going to be threatened by the arrival of a sibling.

The problem with late spacing is that the older child has had time to settle comfortably—too comfortably, in fact—into the role of "only child." That is his territory, so to speak, within the family, and he isn't willing to share it with anyone else.

For the first eight months of the second-born child's life, his relative passivity and helplessness pose few problems for the firstborn. As the baby begins to move about independently and make increasing demands on the parents' time and attention, however, the older child's perception of him begins to change. Where once the baby was cute and cuddly, the older child now begins to see him as an intruder. The firstborn's response to this perceived threat varies according to his temperament and history as well as the spacing between the two. In the case of early spacing, the older child may become agressive toward the baby, or he may regress in one or more ways (e.g., baby talk, wetting his pants, wanting to drink from a bottle) in an attempt to reclaim the attention he's lost. When spacing is late, the older child may exhibit jealousy toward the younger child by ignoring him, refusing to share toys, and teasing.

It's all but inevitable that a toddler will have some difficulty adjusting to a new sibling. Some will have a lot, some just a little. Some start having difficulty several months before the birth of the second child, while others have no problems at all until the baby is crawling. Regardless, problems of one sort or another are almost certain. The good news is they can be minimized with proper planning and management, as in:

• *Involvement:* Include the older child in such things as shopping for baby furniture, decorating the nursery, and talking about names. This will help him feel he's playing an important role in the baby's arrival. The greater his "investment" along these lines, the more likely it is he will develop feelings of affection toward the baby long before the "Big Day."

Once baby has arrived, continue to find ways of engaging the older child's help. This will not only boost his self-esteem, but also prevent the feeling he's competing with the baby for your attention. For the child who's too young to help without getting underfoot, buy a doll and an array of baby things—disposable diapers, a bottle, and a doll crib. If the older child begins clamoring for attention while your hands are full with the baby, say, "I'm feeding the baby. It's time for you to feed your baby, too." The underinvolved child is likely to regard the baby as a trespasser, someone he didn't ask for and doesn't especially want. As a result, he will seek ways of discharging his jealousy. These may range from getting into mischief whenever Mom is occupied with feeding or diapering to actual displays of aggression toward the baby. Behaviors such as these are signals from the child that he's feeling left out and needs not just more attention from his parents, but more involvement with his new sibling as well.

• *Plan Ahead:* Avoid surprises that might result in feelings of anger or frustration on the part of the older child. Don't, for example, suddenly give the older child's room to the baby. Make transitions of this sort several months before the baby's arrival.

• *Talk:* Include the firstborn in discussions about the baby. Let him feel the baby's movements. Borrow a stethoscope and let him hear the baby's heartbeat. Show him pictures of himself when he was a newborn. Talk about the responsibilities he'll have toward his new brother or sister. If, after the baby's arrival, the first child seems to be having problems, it may help to read him a book that deals with this subject. Knowing he's not alone in the world with these feelings will help him come to grips with them. One of the better books of this genre is *Peter's Chair* by Ezra Jack Keats. In it, Peter talks about how mad he is that his baby sister has moved in and taken his crib and favorite chair. This charming little book shows how Peter resolves this crisis.

• *This Is Everybody's Baby!:* The fact that most babies are born away from home makes it difficult for young children to relate to the event. If the hospital has a sibling program, make sure you enroll the older child well in advance. If hospital policy allows, take the older child for a first look at his new baby brother or sister through the nursery window. If these aren't options, at least make sure the older child speaks to Mom by phone a couple of times a day, especially just before bedtime.

Once Mom and baby are home and receiving visitors, encourage friends and relatives to bring a small surprise for the older child, especially if they're coming with a gift for the baby. Also mention to them how important it is that they make a bit of a fuss over the older child as well, congratulating him on how cute *his* baby brother or sister is, and how proud he must be. By taking the simple steps to support the first child's adjustment to the second, you help set a positive tone in the sibling relationship from the very beginning. That means less jealousy now, and less sibling conflict later. Now that's an offer no parent can refuse!

Questions?

Q *What should we look for when selecting toys for our child, who's now twenty-five months old?*

A The concept of "play value" is an important one for parents to keep in mind when selecting toys for children. A toy's "play value" is measured in terms of three characteristics: durability, flexibility, and developmental appropriateness.

Durability: This simply refers to the toy's ability to withstand the wear and tear of a child's play. Since toddlers like to take things apart anyway, it's wise to purchase toys they can take apart without breaking.

Flexibility: A flexible toy can be many things, as opposed to one thing only. Blocks, for example, are flexible, while a wind-up train is not. The more flexible, or multidimensional, the toy, the more it will stimulate the child's imagination and promote creative behavior.

Developmentally appropriate: Does the toy "match" the child's developmental characteristics? Toys that can be disassembled without breaking are developmentally appropriate for toddlers because toddlers like to take things apart. Blocks are developmentally appropriate to toddlers because toddlers like to build things. Crayons are developmentally appropriate for toddlers because toddlers like to create (especially by scribbling). Dolls are developmentally appropriate for older toddlers because older toddlers like to engage in pretend play.

The greater a toy's "play value," the longer it will hold a child's interest. It follows that by choosing toys that are high in "play value," parents can save money along with promoting their children's development.

Q *What should I look for when choosing books for my two-year-old?*

A More than anything else, you should look for books that interest *you*—books that attract your attention and that you will enjoy reading yourself. The more you enjoy a book, the more enthusiasm you will bring to the act of reading it aloud. The more enthusiasm you bring, the more you will stimulate your child's imagination and language skills, and the more effectively you will communicate to your child the most important message of all: Reading is fun!

In addition, look for books that are durable, colorful, and written in short, simple, yet interesting sentences. In that last regard, keep in mind that toddlers are captivated by rhyme, which is why the Dr. Seuss books are so enduringly popular with children this age.

When reading to your child, bring the story to life by modulating your tone of voice. Consider taking on a different voice for each character, even singing parts of the book. Also, once your child learns the story, stop at the last word or phrase of certain sentences, letting your child fill it in. Interactive reading of this sort is just another way of hooking your child on books, and the earlier he's hooked, the better.

Q *Our first child is eighteen months old. When should we begin reading to her?*

A About a year ago. Seriously, folks, a child is never too young to be read to. Parents should begin reading to a child at least by six months, but if you had started reading to your daughter when she was a few days old, it would have been even better.

"But she wouldn't have been able to see the pictures!"

So what? Since when are pictures necessary to reading? Either my mother or grandmother read to me every night before bed until I was at least six years old. The selections included *The Wind in the Willows*, folk tales by Andersen and the Brothers Grimm, *The Jungle Book*, and other children's classics, none of which had more than a picture every twenty pages or so. I didn't know any better, so I never complained. But I did pay attention. And I did use my imagination.

In bygone days, however, when reading to my children, I generally preferred books with lots and lots of pictures because that forced us to cuddle. The pictures also became the occasion for games of "Show me . . ." and "What's this?"

Early reading stimulates language development, imagination, and cognitive growth. In addition, studies have shown that as a child's communication skills improve, so does motor coordination. This makes sense, not only because an enriching environment stimulates a child's abilities in all areas, but also because language development and motor behavior are interwoven during early childhood. The nurturing that takes place when a parent reads to a child also helps strengthen the child's sense of security, which in turn contributes greatly to the development of independence.

Security, independence, intellectual competence—these are the ingredients that go into the making of self-esteem. So you see, early (and ongoing) reading is one of the best investments you can make toward your child's well-being.

Don't, however, confuse the purpose of early reading with teaching a child to read. When you sit down to read to your daughter, do so because it's something you both enjoy. If you start reading to her now, and read to her often, she will learn that reading is enjoyable, and that is sufficient. It isn't unusual for a well-read-to child, at age three or four, to suddenly begin reading. With enough exposure, some children figure the rules out on their own. If they don't, and learn to read in the first few grades of elementary school, that's okay too.

Q We are the parents of a perfectly happy, outgoing boy of fifteen months. We regularly dress in front of him and take baths with him. Up until now, Herman hasn't acted overly interested in our private parts, but we'd like some guidance for the future. Is there a point at which we should stop appearing nude in front of him? How should we answer him when he asks questions about our bodies? When he's four or five, but still needs help with his bath, will he be embarrassed to have us bathe him?

A Here are the bare facts: At this age, there's no harm in what you're doing with and in front of Herman. At some point in the near future, he will surely become interested in your "private parts." When he asks, "What's this?" answer him as casually as if he pointed to your chin.

Concerning what to call these body parts, there are those who insist that parents should answer with none other than proper anatomical terms. Rest assured, excepting vulgarities, there's nothing to fret over either way. Words like "winky" and "bum-bum" are perfectly okay and no more misleading than calling the child's stomach a "tummy."

Sometime between his third and fourth birthdays, Herman will begin developing what's known as "gender identity." He will realize that girls and boys are physically different and that not only is he a boy, but he is like his daddy in this respect. The fact that you have been casual to this point concerning nudity will help him make this important distinction and realize also that he has nothing of which to be ashamed.

This is, however, the appropriate time to introduce the concept of modesty. From this point on, you should be more circumspect about appearing nude in front of Herman. I'm not suggesting that you become neurotic about nudity, just prudent. After all, it's impossible for several people to live together in close quarters without seeing at least occasional glimpses of one another's unadorned bodies.

The older Herman gets, the more you should expect him to respect your privacy, and likewise, the more you should respect his. Nonetheless, there's never anything wrong with the occasional incidental glimpses of other nude bodies that are bound to happen in any family.

Four is a good age at which to discontinue the practice of taking baths with Herman. You can use the excuse that he's too big for the both of you to fit comfortably in the tub at the same time. By the by, I don't think Herman would be at all embarrassed for you to bathe him when he's four or five, but you shouldn't have to. A four-year-old can shut the drain, turn on faucets, mix the water temperatures properly, shut the faucets off, and soap, rinse, and dry himself. Some supervision may be necessary, but a four-year-old should be pretty much on his own where taking a bath is concerned.

Q *We are very health-conscious parents who want our eighteen-month-old daughter to grow up physically fit. There's an exercise program for toddlers at a local health club, and we'd like to know your feelings about such things.*

A Exercise programs for toddlers, eh? Aren't toddlers active enough as it is? I know mine were. By the time they were eighteen months old, they were climbing bookcases, escaping from their cribs, jumping on furniture, throwing food, and running away from us in stores, airports, and other crowded places. They got plenty of exercise, and so did we.

Who needs more active babies? None of the parents I know. Maybe there are a lot of fat, lethargic babies in California, where (predictably) the baby exercise idea got its start, but there aren't many where I live.

Not only are baby exercise programs unnecessary, they're downright dangerous to the mental health of parents! I can see it now: As the baby exercise craze sweeps the nation, we begin hearing reports of nine-month-olds vaulting out of their playpens, twelve-month-olds escaping down crib-sheet ropes from their bedroom windows, and eighteen-month-olds running merrily through the streets of America with their parents in hot, panting pursuit; going slowly, but aerobically insane.

Yes, infants and toddlers should get plenty of exercise. And yes, they will, pretty much on their own, as long as parents and other caregivers provide environments that are safe, stimulating, and allow for plenty of movement, exploration, and manipulation. Baby exercise classes are no substitute for a home that recognizes the growing child's need for activity and, within reasonable boundaries, allows for it.

If a youngster isn't able to get enough exercise at home, exercise classes won't even put a drop in the bucket of his exercise needs. On the other hand, if the child is getting enough exercise at home, then the structure of an exercise class will be an uncreative waste of the child's time. And parents who are worried about their children "becoming all they can be" should keep in mind that when you waste a child's time, you also waste his potential.

Q *Our daughter, who just turned two, has started asking me "Why?" about almost everything. She'll ask me a question like, "What's this?" (pointing to a picture in a book). I'll answer and she'll ask "Why?" I don't want her to stop asking questions, but sometimes I feel like a nonstop answer machine. How should I be handling this?*

A You must first realize that simply because your daughter can ask the question "Why?" doesn't mean she can understand the answer. For instance, let's say she points to a picture of the sun going down and asks, "What's this?" You say, "It's a picture of the sun going down," to which she asks, "Why?" I guarantee that no amount of explaining will cause her to understand why the sun seems to disappear over the edge of the earth every evening. At age two, she's probably unable to comprehend the answers to very few of her "Why?" questions. But as you've discovered, comprehend or not, she's going to keep on asking.

The never-ending "Why?" is typical of intelligent two-year-olds. It is, first, a request for information. As such, you should give information, but it isn't necessary that the information be scientifically correct. In fact, your answer can be total fiction as long as it relates in some way to the original question. For example, if your daughter asks why the sun goes down, you can answer, "Because it's tired and needs to sleep," or "Because it's playing peekaboo with you." One answer is really as good as the next. It's even all right to give a different answer every time your daughter asks the same question!

Your daughter keeps asking "Why?" because she is beginning to understand cause-and-effect. This is an exciting discovery, and she wants to know as much about it as she can! It's enough, however, that you simply confirm for her that "Yes, there's a reason for that, too!" In addition, it's important that the answer be in terms she *can* understand. In most cases, that eliminates the "correct" answer from the running.

If you think that what I'm suggesting is tantamount to "lying" to her, take a look at the books you read to her. In them, there are fantastic creatures and trees that talk and all manner of impossible things. The point is, it's not necessary that you describe the world to young children in correct terms; only that you describe it in terms they can relate to and comprehend. If it was vital that young children always hear correct answers and descriptions, we'd read to them from the encyclopedia instead of a storybook.

Realize, also, that the repetitive "why?" is the beginning of conversation. It's verbal give-and-take at it's most basic level. And again, the give-and-take, the process, is far more important than the content of your answers. When you've had enough, change the subject by asking *her* a question or giving her something to do.

Q *Our first child, an eighteen-month-old daughter, has recently started clinging to me (her mother), following me from room to room, and wanting to be held more than ever. I thought children became more independent as they got older. Have I done something to make her insecure?*

A Children *do* become more independent as they get older, but sometimes independence grows in a two-steps-forward, one-step-backward fashion. This is one of those times.

Envision yourself venturing to explore a dark, deserted house, one that has both attracted and repelled you with its mystery. You open the door and stand there for a while until your eyes adjust to the dim light. Then you take a few steps into the house and stop. Hearing a creak, you retreat back to the front door until you are reassured that all is safe. Taking a few more steps into the house than before, you once again stop and listen. Then you take a few more steps, and again you stop. Every time you hear something that sets your heart pounding, you retreat to the last "safe" place you occupied until the coast is again clear.

And so it goes with your daughter, who has begun the process of self-discovery. Up until now, she has not had a sense of her own identity. As self-consciousness begins to develop and the drive toward independence awakens, she is thrown into conflict. To become a person in her own right, she must leave the safety of her relationship with you and venture into uncharted, yet compelling territory. Intuitively she knows that once those steps are taken, nothing will ever again be the same between you. Before she puts this distance between herself and you, she must first be absolutely certain that you will still be there whenever she feels the need for reassurance.

No, you haven't made your daughter insecure. In order to achieve a state of independence, she must learn to accept and deal with insecurity. Research has shown that the more available and reassuring mothers are during this stage, the better. Even though your daughter's clinging and following may, at times, be oppressive, it's best to allow it. A child who has trouble getting back "Home" again, won't want to leave. Let her cling, and she will eventually cling less. Let her follow, and she will follow less. Hold her when she wants, and she will eventually ask to be held less. Believe me, there'll come a day when you'll wish she asked you to hold her more often.

Q *My thirty-three-month-old daughter has suddenly developed a fear of going outside. If I try to take her outside to play, go for a walk, or even go down the street to see a friend, she begins to scream. She isn't able to tell me what she's afraid of, nor do I have a clue. I'm home with her during the day and nothing traumatic has happened that might explain this. Do you have some idea as to what might be going on here?*

A The sudden onset of strange and inexplicable fears is not at all unusual in older toddlers and threes. The parent of an almost-three-year-old once told me her son had become deathly afraid of newspapers and would flee hysterically from any room in which he discovered one. Other parents have recounted equally peculiar stories of older toddlers developing fears of birds, bushes, flashlights, and running water. Then, of course, there are the usual fears of the dark, thunder, and dogs.

All of this is normal, I assure you. The child's imagination—the first stirring of abstract thought—is beginning to flower at this age. Previously, things were exactly as they seemed. Outside was outside, newspapers were newspapers. Now, however, as imagination begins to play games with pure sensory experience, perception becomes a matter of interpretation. Outside becomes a threatening place, and newspapers—perhaps because of the crinkling, popping noises of their pages being turned—become living things capable of who knows what. We can romanticize this leap of consciousness as mind-expanding (and accurately so), but the fact remains it introduces a dimension to the child's perception of reality that can be frightening.

Your daughter needs to feel a sense of absolute confidence in your ability to control a world that's suddenly become threatening. You must act as if you know exactly what you're doing. Accept her fears, but do not participate in them. Don't ask her why she's afraid. She won't be able to tell you, and whatever words you put in her mouth will only worsen her anxieties. Don't discredit her fears, either, by saying "That's silly" or things along those lines.

If she suddenly tells you she's afraid of monsters, don't tell her there's no such thing. This age child cannot understand why a word exists for something that does not. If she wants to talk about what's frightening her, just listen. When it's your turn to talk, say, "Everything's all right. Mommy and Daddy are here to take care of you, and we will!"

The only way she's going to stop being afraid is if you help her confront the very thing she fears most. If you don't have to leave the house for any other purpose during the day, take her on a walk around the neighborhood. Don't ask if she wants to go, just take her. If she screams, just hold her and remind her that everything's all right, that you are taking care of her. Given an adequate display of control on your part, this crisis will run its course in short order.

Q *Our thirty-four-month-old son has suddenly become afraid of the dark. He won't stay in his bedroom at night because he thinks there's a monster under his bed. Our solution has been to let him fall asleep on the sofa and move him to his bed when he's asleep. A psychiatrist acquaintance of ours said this was an "obvious manipulation" on our son's part, an "attempt to control us." What do you think?*

A I think the statement made by the psychiatrist is an obvious manipulation on his part, an attempt on his part to control *you.* Some people invent monsters for themselves, some invent them for other people.

Fears are common to this age child. Leading the list is a fear of the dark, including the belief that malevolent creatures lurk therein. At this age, fears result from the interaction of three related factors:

• *The need to protect a fragile sense of identity.* As a child grows in self-sufficiency, he must learn to handle the anxiety that comes with letting go of his parents. Fears dramatize this process. They are symbolic, fantasy-driven expressions of the young child's emotional vulnerability.

• *The flowering of imaginative thought.* This age child is able to conjure up mental images of things real and unreal, but isn't able to discriminate between the two. Whatever he can see in his mind is no less real to him than the things he sees in his front yard.

• *The inseparability of word and thing.* In the mind of an older toddler, if something has a name, then it must exist. The idea that there are words for things that don't exist is incomprehensible to this age child. This is why any attempt to talk a toddler or three-year-old out of fears won't work. The rational explanation and the fear are on separate wavelengths.

Problems concerning a young child's fears arise because parents often misinterpret them as expressions of insecurity or upcoming emotional problems. The parents then begin responding to the child's fears with guilt and anxiety. Their attempts to compensate for the "damage" simply increase the child's confusion and sense of helplessness. The more anxious the parents become, the more fearful the child becomes. Their reactions reinforce the fear and confirm it as something real. If there is nothing to be afraid of, thinks the child, then why are Mommy and Daddy acting so afraid?

The most effective approach is first, acknowledge the fear ("I know the dark can be scary when you're little"). Second, identify with your son ("When I was little, I was afraid, too"). Third, reassure your son of your ability to protect him. You can also help him overcome his fright by playing upon the talent that created it—namely, his imagination. Have him relax and look at a blank wall. Then, tell him to think about a tall, handsome prince on a beautiful white horse (be very descriptive). Say, "This prince, named Jedclampett, is your friend. If you call his name, he will come into your room and chase the monster away. While you sleep, he will stand guard over your bed and keep the monster away." Use *your* imagination to elaborate on this or any similar idea and plant it firmly in your son's mind.

Farfetched? Not to a young child. If he can conjure up a monster, he can conjure up a guardian prince. And have lots of fun, to boot!

Q *Our thirty-two-month-old daughter has recently invented an imaginary playmate whom she calls "Cindy." Her obsession with this new friend is going a bit far, I think. She sometimes wants me to set a place at the table for Cindy and never fails to bring her along any time we leave the house. When I've suggested that Cindy isn't real, my daughter has become angry and upset, so I've dropped it. Do I have reason to be concerned, or is this just a passing phase?*

A Your daughter's fascination with Cindy is just a passing phase, but a very important one. Rather than being worried, you should be glad. Fantasy thinking emerges in the late twos or early threes. Like any other mental attribute, imagination must be exercised in order to strengthen and grow. Cindy provides your daughter with the opportunity to do just that. This is a very important step toward the eventual mastery of abstract thinking ability. Also, since imagination is essential to reading comprehension, Cindy is actually helping your daughter toward becoming a successful reader.

Trying to debate the issue of Cindy's existence with your daughter is a lost cause. In your daughter's eyes and mind, Cindy is as real as you are. Furthermore, young children invest a considerable amount of security in their imaginary playmates. They *need* them. No wonder your daughter became upset when you denied Cindy's existence. Just as your adult mind cannot comprehend your daughter's obsession with Cindy, your daughter cannot comprehend your failure to accept her. So, call it a draw and stop worrying.

Cindy is also helping your daughter develop social skills. This is timely, because at this age, your daughter is beginning to form relationships with other children. Cindy enables her to practice social skills in a safe, nonthreatening context.

The more your daughter plays with Cindy, the fewer demands she makes of you. Instead of relying on you for occupation, she is relying on Cindy, which effectively means she is relying on herself. The more self-reliant and resourceful your daughter becomes, the better sense of self-esteem she will have.

Any way you look at it, Cindy is one of the best things that's ever happened to your daughter. Her invisible friend is contributing to almost every aspect of her growth and development. Instead of worrying about her "obsession," relax and count your blessings.

Q *We have a son who's nearly three and an eight-month-old daughter. All of a sudden, our son wants to drink from a bottle, wear diapers during the day, and be rocked to sleep. Despite several tantrums, we haven't given in to these demands. Now he's started wetting his pants during the day, something he hasn't done in six months. What should we do about this?*

A Your job is to reassure your son that his place in the family, while different and changing, is still secure and protected. You must also convince him, firmly but gently, that the time for bottles, being rocked to sleep, and wearing diapers has passed. The next time he wets his pants, have him help you clean up the "spill." Then, take him to the bathroom and teach him to rinse out his wet clothing and drape it over the tub to dry. This isn't punishment, and you shouldn't communicate it as such. Furthermore, you needn't be overly concerned with how good a job he does. You are only making him responsible for his accident and showing him you won't give in on the diaper issue.

Q We have two children, ages five and two, with a third on the way. Which of the two children is more likely to have problems with the new arrival, and what, if anything, can we do to prevent them?

A Your two-year-old will have to make more of an adjustment to the new sibling than the five-year-old. The reason for this is simple: When the third child arrives, the five-year-old will retain his status—that of oldest child—but for the two-year-old, everything will change. He will have to relinquish his role as the "baby" to his new brother or sister and become instead the middle child. This shuffling of roles causes what amounts to an identity crisis and often results in the attention-seeking behavior characteristic of "middle child syndrome." A study in conflict and contradiction, the middle child ends up wanting the best of both his older and younger siblings' worlds. He wants the freedom and privilege given the oldest, as well as the attention given the youngest. To keep this syndrome at a minimum, involve the two-year-old as much as possible in preparing for the third child's arrival. Once he or she is here, find ways your two-year-old can help you take care of the baby. The more important you make him feel in his own right, the less he'll strive for attention in inappropriate ways.

Q Our thirty-month-old has recently started hitting, pushing, and squeezing his ten-month-old sister. What's causing this and how should we handle it?

A Your son's aggression results from a combination of jealousy, territorial instincts, and clumsy attempts to play with his sister. Your first order of business is to protect the baby. Your second is to guide your son into a more gentle relationship with his sister. Begin by putting her completely off-limits to your son. For at least a week, don't allow him to hold, touch, or even come near her. During this time, however, have him help you by getting things and doing things for you while you're involved with the baby. After a week or so, begin allowing your son brief moments of closely supervised contact with his sister—getting toys for her, helping you change her, and so on. Praise him for being gentle and helpful. As time goes on, increase the number and kind of contact you allow him to have with her. If your son hurts the baby, sit him in a "time-out" chair for a few minutes. If he says he's sorry, simply say, "I know you are, but you must learn to be gentle with your baby sister." This will almost certainly be a two-steps-forward, one-step-back process for at least several weeks. Eventually, however, your patience and consistency will pay off. (See chapter 6 for more on this subject.)

Q My husband and I separated several months ago. Ever since, our usually outgoing, happy, thirty-four-month-old daughter has been clinging and whiny. She wants to be with me all the time. If I tell her to stop following me around, she begins to cry. Almost every day, she asks when her daddy is coming back. He's not, but I'm worried that the truth will upset her even more. What should I be doing to help her through this crisis?

A Following a separation, young children will often cling almost desperately to the remaining parent. Preschoolers—boys as well as girls—tend to be more dependent upon their mothers than their fathers. Nevertheless, your husband's presence in the home was essential to your daughter's "picture" of the family as a constant, unchanging unit. Her father's departure altered this picture and disrupted, therefore, her sense of security. In response, she clings to you as if to say, "Don't you leave me, too!"

This is no doubt an extremely vulnerable time for you as well. Your security has been turned upside down, and your emotional resources are stretched to their limit. Under the circumstances, it may be difficult for you to respond patiently to your daughter's overpowering need for reassurance. A vicious cycle may be developing: the more anxious you are, the more anxious your daughter becomes; the more insecure she acts, the more anxious you become; and so on. If you feel caught up in this cycle, it may be wise for you to see an experienced family counselor. A competent professional can help you restabilize your new family situation.

Under the circumstances, it isn't unusual for a child to regress to behaviors typical of earlier stages of growth— behaviors associated with safety and security. Your daughter's clinging is one example of this. If she wants to be held, and you can hold her, hold her. If, at the moment, you cannot hold her, tell her why and try to redirect her attention to something else until your hands are free. In other words, be as responsive as you can possibly be to her, but don't let her take control of the relationship.

Answer her questions clearly and honestly. Don't editorialize about the separation. Just stick to the facts. Tell her that Daddy is going to live somewhere else, but don't try to explain why. Tell her what role her daddy will continue to play in her life, and remember that he will continue to play an important role in your life, as well. In the long run, the best thing for your daughter is two parents who do their best to put aside their animosities and make every effort to communicate often and well.

Q *My husband and I are on the verge of a separation that probably will be permanent. We have agreed I will have primary custody of our two-year-old son. My main concern: Our little boy has developed a close relationship with his father. I am concerned that separating them at this time may do our son emotional harm. What advice do you have for us?*

A If you and your husband are doing what you feel is best for the both of you, it is also the best thing to do where your son is concerned. Ultimately, a well-thought-out and amicable separation will do far less harm to him than the stress of witnessing conflict and the absence of a loving relationship between his parents over a prolonged period of time.

This change is likely to temporarily disrupt your son's sense of security. He may respond by becoming more clinging, irritable, and less tolerant of frustration. He may also regress in his toileting, eating, or sleeping habits. Behavioral changes of this sort can be minimized by explaining the separation to him in simple, concrete terms the day of his father's move. The more of a dramatic buildup you give the situation, the more unsettled your son is likely to become. How quickly and successfully he recovers his sense of security depends on three factors:

• How successfully the two of you adjust to the separation. If either or both of you convey to your son that the separation is emotionally traumatic, his feelings of insecurity will be heightened.

• How well you handle negative feelings toward one another. If either of you is embittered by the separation, you are likely to communicate that unwittingly to your son. This will generate feelings of confusion, threatening his self-worth.

• How regularly his father visits with your son. If practical considerations prevent regular visitation, his father should call and write (also consider recording cassette tapes) often. The predictability of contact with the absent parent is important to maintaining an open, trusting relationship.

Q My nineteen-month-old son bites me several times a day, sometimes because he's clearly mad at me, but sometimes for no reason whatsoever. I've spanked him, put him in his crib, and—at the advice of my pediatrician—bit him back. Nothing has worked, and I can't figure out why he's doing this. I'm worried that perhaps I've done something to cause this, but can't figure out what. What should I do now?

A You're taking this too personally. He not biting you because he has negative feelings toward you. He's biting you because you're *there*. You frustrate him more than anyone else because you share more time with him than does anyone else. Throw in the fact that toddlers are easily frustrated, have no self-control to speak of, and love to sink their chops into things, and you have a typical nineteen-month-old biting his typical mother.

Your son bites you at different times for different reasons, but he continues to bite because you've never really insisted that he stop. Dwelling on the "why?" of his biting has distracted you from your job, which is to communicate your clear disapproval of biting. Put yourself squarely in the present tense and *do* something. As much as possible, prevent his toothy attacks, even those that seem merely playful. I'll just bet you can tell, nine out of ten times, when a bite is on the way. Every time he tries to bite you, face him and say "No!" Then, turning him away from you so he can't bite again, take him to his room, put him down on the floor (not in his crib), and walk away, leaving the door open as you leave. If you do this every time he bites or tries to bite, he will eventually get the message.

When he learns that you're no longer a target, he may try biting someone else. Again, whether or not you're able to prevent that from happening, go through the same sequence. If you aren't at home, improvise with an out-of-the-way chair. By the way, biting a child back sometimes works, but more often it makes the problems worse. Because parents are now modeling the behavior they want stopped, it can confuse the child or start a let's-see-who-can-bite-harder contest.

Q   I'm having trouble getting my twenty-month-old son to give up drinking from a bottle. He drinks from a cup at meals and during the day, but cries for his bottle whenever he's upset or sleepy. Should I refuse to give it to him?

A   There is much to lose and nothing to be gained by struggling with yor son over whether he can have his bottle when he feels the need for it. When we make issues out of things like bottles and thumbs and security blankets, children are likely to become more desperate in their attachment to them. Allow your son to drink from a bottle whenever he expresses the need for that source of comfort. Insist, however, that he follow your lead and drink from a cup during meals. Don't fill his bottle with milk or sugar-sweetened liquids, as these will increase the risk of early tooth decay. Fill it with unsweetened (strained) fruit juice or water only. A nonchallant approach will result in your son losing interest in the bottle in a relatively short period of time.

Security blankets, thumbs, pacifiers, and the like are known as *transitional objects*. They help young children feel secure enough to make the leap from one level of development to the next. Despite the prejudiced view parents tend to have of them, these sorts of things are actually a parent's best friend. A child who carries a security blanket with him to preschool is more likely to separate easily from parents. A child who's allowed to suck his thumb is self-comforting when frustrated.

It may, at times, make practical sense to limit a child's access to transitional objects, but children will give them up more quickly if parents don't prohibit them altogether. For example, parents might tell a child he can carry his security blanket to preschool, but must give it to the teacher once he arrives. Likewise, parents might tell a child he can have his pacifier only at nap time and bedtime. In any case, a child is not going to lose interest in a transitional object as long as his or her parents act as if it's the biggest deal in the world.

Q *Our daughter is nearly three. She's sucked her thumb since the day she was born. The dentist assures us that she isn't sucking hard enough to cause a serious orthodontic problem, so we aren't in a panic over it. Basically, we allow her to suck whenever she wants to, which is mostly when she's bored or upset. Lately, however, we've become concerned that perhaps our permissiveness might backfire on her when she gets to school and encounters ridicule and criticism from other children and maybe even teachers. Should we begin now to try to stop her thumb sucking, and if so, how?*

A If your daughter's thumb sucking isn't resulting in dental problems, and if it hasn't been a battle up until now, why make it one? And a battle is what you'll surely have if you try to make her stop.

My daughter, Amy, also sucked her thumb from birth and probably, if the truth were known, for some time before she was born. She didn't apply pressure to the roof of her mouth and no dental problems ensued. When Amy went to school, even though she'd never heard criticism about her habit from us, she seemed to sense that it wasn't something other people would look kindly upon. So, she restrained herself from thumb sucking during school hours. In retrospect, I'm fairly certain that if we had been critical of her thumb sucking, Amy would not have stopped as she even-

tually did. Instead, she would have developed an immunity
to criticism and not cared about what the peer group thought
about what she did with her thumb. If your parents have
already made you feel as bad as you possibly can feel about
something so harmless, why should you care what anyone
else thinks or says about it?

My theory is that the more parents try to stop a child from
thumb sucking, the more determined the child becomes,
and the more pressure the child will apply to the palate,
thereby increasing the chances of future orthodontic problems. So don't try to stop your daughter from sucking her
thumb. She enjoys it, it's harmless, and she uses her thumb
to comfort herself when she's upset. When she begins school,
she'll become quickly aware of and responsive to what her
peers think of her habit.

The only negative thing we ever said to Amy about her
thumb sucking was "We can't understand you, Miss Amy,
when you talk to us with your thumb in your mouth." There
are times when one simply must be practical.

Chapter 3

Creative Discipline

"M y eighteen-month-old gets into everything and manages to stay two steps ahead of me, no matter what I do!" said her mother, looking bedraggled, as parents of toddlers often do. "She hits the deck running in the morning and, her nap aside, keeps me going until her bedtime, which comes none too soon."

"I suppose our two-and-a-half-year-old son is what you'd call a strong-willed child," his father told me, as if finally willing to speak the unspeakable. "Anytime things don't go his way, he flops on the floor and begins to scream and thrash about. If we try to comfort him, he scratches, hits, pulls our hair, tries to bite us. It's this Jekyll and Hyde thing. One minute he's this lovable, playful kid; the next, he's the Son of Satan."

"Last month, my two-year-old suddenly decided he was no longer going to do anything I asked," his mother complained, dark circles under her eyes. "If I tell him *not* to do something, he does it, all the while looking at me with this gleam in his eye. If I tell him to *stop* doing something, he keeps right on doing it. If I tell him to *do* something, he looks at me like I've got my nerve and says, 'No!' That's all, just 'No!'"

These parents' woeful tales are the stuff of life with toddlers. They get into everything, they scream when they don't get their way, they do what you tell 'em not to do and won't do what you tell 'em *to* do. Not all two-year-olds are like this, mind you. Some are sweet and lovable all their days, forever and ever, amen. My theory is that these rare children are really aliens from another planet who are hiding in the bodies of human children and trying their best not to draw attention to themselves. But your typical toddler earns his age-group's reputation for terribleness. All this running amok and screaming and stubbornness is intimidating to parents, even downright scary. I remember, when Eric was this age, thinking he was neuropsychologically and biochemically defective; that by early adulthood he was going to be either in lifelong solitary confinement in a maximum-security prison or in a stainless steel straitjacket in some equally maximum-security nuthouse. And in my darkest fantasies, there was nothing we could do about it.

Some parents react to this intimidation, this scariness, by caving in. They get into this perpetual-motion routine of trying to figure out what will make their children happy. They think, you see, that good parents have happy children. So, to verify their own wonderfulness, they do whatever it takes to keep their children on an even keel. In no time flat, these children are in complete control of their families.

Other parents react to this intimidation by trying to outintimidate their children. They scream, brandish belts, threaten to spank, spank, scream, threaten to spank, spank, and so on. When their children are in their early teens, these parents are still screaming and threatening to spank and spanking. They never get anywhere because they never learn. Their children? Who knows? The lucky ones, perhaps because of understanding grandparents or teachers, make it. Human children are, after all, incredibly resilient. The not-so-lucky ones . . . well, who knows?

In both cases, these parents take their children's screaming and stubbornness personally. The first group appeases and caters because they think they've done something *wrong* to make their children act this way. They're trying to make up for their supposed wrongdoing. The second group consists of parents who take their children's behavior as a personal affront, a symptom of ingratitude or something. They're determined to punish this ingratitude into oblivion.

Before we go any further, let's get something straight. This behavior, no matter how extreme, is normal for this age. We're talking about children who think they're the center of the universe, for gosh sakes. From their charming but thoroughly deluded point of view, no one has a right to tell them what to do, or deny them what they want, or even delay giving it to them.

If you thought you were the center of the universe, and the people in your life had been cooperating in that psychosis for however long, and then everyone decided to stop cooperating and begin describing the world to you in realistic terms, you'd scream, too. And you'd refuse to acknowledge they were right. You'd be that much more demanding and uncooperative and generally difficult to live with.

So, our two-year-old, before he can accept that he is *not* the center of the universe, must make one last-ditch, pull-out-all-the-stops effort to assert that he is! Such is life, folks. Things always get worse before they get better, remember? It's our job to demonstrate to the child, firmly but gently, that he isn't.

If you understand why two-year-olds act the way they do, there's no reason to become either intimidated or angry. Understanding enables acceptance. If you accept it, then this, too, will pass. If you can't accept it, this behavior—in one way, shape, or form—will be an issue forever. Furthermore, the only way you can successfully steer a two-year-old toward cooperation, creativity, and self-control is to understand and accept. Unfettered of anxiety and anger, you can see the big picture, communicate clearly, position yourself properly, keep your balance, and do the job God wants you to do and mankind *needs* you to do.

It's called discipline, and it's really not that complicated. With two-year-olds, there are three important disciplinary goals:

• First, you want to set limits that contain your child's behavior but that do not interfere with the growth of mastery (competence).

• Second, you want to help your child develop both the ability to delay gratification and tolerate frustration (one and the same, really).

• Third, you want to convince your child that you are in control of his world, thus capable of providing for and protecting him under any and all circumstances. To convince a two-year-old that you are in control of the world, you must first demonstrate that you are in control of him. To demonstrate to a two-year-old that you are in control of him, you must demonstrate that you are in control of yourself.

To accomplish these objectives, you need three tools:

• First, you need to manage your child's environment properly.
• Second, you need to communicate properly.
• Third, you need to be *proactive*, as opposed to *reactive*, concerning problems.

Environmental Management

Remember, at the beginning of this chapter, the eighteen-month-old who was always on the go, getting into everything? So what's new? His mother's plaintive description fits the typical, full-steam-ahead toddler. The solution is environmental management. The centerpiece of our solution is called *child-proofing*.

Toddlers are intensely inquisitive beings. They want to know what it is, how it works, what it can do, how it comes apart, and what it takes to break it. Exploring and experimenting are the name of the game, otherwise known as getting into things. There is no other way for a toddler to answer all the questions that come to mind. He doesn't have the words with which to ask the questions, so he acts them out. Every new discovery raises more questions than it answers, thus further stimulating the child's curiosity. The more the toddler finds out, in other words, the more he wants to know.

As the child's interest in his environment expands, parents should appreciate and respond to his need to explore by providing an environment that is both stimulating and safe. The most economical way of doing this, as well as the most sensible, is by child-proofing. Child-proofing a home shouldn't take more than a few hours and generally costs less than twenty dollars.

Begin by taking inventory, a room at a time, of things dangerous or valuable that are within the child's reach. Keep in mind that if your child isn't yet climbing, he soon will be. Put child-proof latches on cabinets (especially lower ones), childproof covers on electrical sockets, and sturdy gates across any open staircases.

At the same time, bring down to the child's level things he can touch, explore, and experiment upon. Give him a cabinet of his own in the kitchen and stock it with things like wooden spoons, pots, empty thread spools, boxes, flexible straws, and any other simple, yet fascinating (from the child's point of view), things. If you do a good job, your child should be able to roam around the house with far less supervision than was previously necessary.

It never fails, when I explain the advantages of child-proofing to parents of toddlers, someone will ask how a child learns to discriminate between what he can and can't touch if parents remove the "can't touch" stuff from reach, if not sight. This misses the point entirely. Parents who child-proof are not giving in to their children; they are accommodating their children's need to exercise curiosity and thus strengthen their minds.

Parents who refuse to child-proof, who view this issue of getting into things as a test of wills, will end up frustrating themselves as well as their child. The child, enraged because the same two people he depends upon are standing in the way of his need to know, discover, and expand his mind, throws tantrums, hits and destroys things, and refuses to cooperate at every turn.

Realize also that young toddlers are fairly incapable of discriminating between "can't touch" and "can touch." The ability to do so won't emerge until sometime around the middle of the third year of life (thirty months, give or take a couple), at which point parents can begin slowly restoring the home to its previous state. To do so, introduce one valuable at a time, first letting the child see and feel the item. When the child's curiosity seems satisfied, put it where it belongs and let the child know it's not a plaything. As long as parents don't introduce too many interesting things at once, the child will usually cooperate with the boundaries being set.

Here's a tip for parents of toddlers when a child of this age picks up something fragile, like a piece of valuable crystal: The child is almost certain to throw the item down if an adult puts on a horrified expression, shouts "No! Give me that!" and moves rapidly, and threateningly, toward the child with arms outstretched, hands open like menacing claws. Panic breeds panic. Instead, control your anxiety, stay in one spot, squat down so you're at eye level with the child, put a smile on your face, extend your hand palm up, and say, "Oooooh, how pretty! Will you put it in my hand so I can see, too?" If you do a good acting job, the child will smile in return and place the item gently in your palm. Let the child know this wasn't a trick by drawing him into your lap and examining the object together for a minute or so. Then, get up and say, "I'm going to put this up here so we can both look at it. Isn't it pretty?" This procedure satisfies the child's curiosity, saves money, and helps build a cooperative, rather than antagonistic, parent-child relationship.

The second important aspect of environmental management involves the aptly termed "boob tube." The best of all worlds for a toddler is a world in which no television exists to distract the child's curiosity from real things and depress the child's intellect. This, of course, means taking the all-but-unheard-of step of removing the television from the family room, if not the house. But if you simply can't comprehend a life without television (or without a television at least close at hand) for yourself, then at least reduce the time it's on when your child is awake to no more than thirty minutes a day.

You may think television is doing you a favor by keeping your dervish from whirling while it's on, but you're sadly mistaken. Televison watching prevents him from learning to occupy his time creatively and constructively. The more, therefore, you use the television set to occupy him, the more likely it becomes that when the television isn't on, or doesn't interest him at that moment, he's going to pester you. The more you use television to free up time for yourself, the more dependent upon the television he—and you—will become.

Besides, you want him to grow up with all the smarts he was born with, don't you? In order to activate those smarts, and keep them activated, a child needs to be *active*. The more opportunity a toddler has to explore and experiment on the environment, the smarter he will become. My formula for a Smart Kid consists of what I refer to as the "Six E's of Excellence": *Expose* the child to *Environments* and *Experiences* that *Enable Exploration* and *Experimentation*. In that context, folks, television simply fails to cut the proverbial mustard. Television produces an electronic environment that depresses exploration and experimentation. For proof of what I'm saying, simply take up station (no pun intended) and watch a child watch television. See the blank expression? See the listless hands? See the lack of any creative, constructive behavior? You're looking at a child wasting time, and time is all the human mind has in which to develop its potential for genius.

The time between a child's birth and seventh birthday (some say sixth, some eighth, so seventh will do) are known as the *formative years*. These are the years during which the child's competency skills are in formation. These skills—verbal, perceptual-motor, intellectual, social, creative—are programmed into the human embryo at the moment of conception. From the moment of birth on, all that's needed to release that potential is generous exposure to environments and experiences that enable exploration and experimentation. That's right, those same Six E's of Excellence. The more the Six E's abound in a child's life, the more excellent, in every sense of the term, he or she will become.

A survey once found that gifted children (truly gifted, as opposed to "gifted" in terms of discriminatory public school definitions) watch an average of less than five hours of television a week during their preschool years. Compare that with a national average of twenty-five hours a week (beginning around the second birthday), and you can begin to appreciate what a drain on the brain the idiot-box truly is.

Besides all this, if you child-proof your home such that your child can explore and experiment to his or her heart's content, thus requiring little supervision, you will not have a toddler who's pestering you constantly to "do for me! do for me!" This is a toddler who'll be too busy doing for himself.

The third aspect of environmental management involves toys. There are two kinds of toys: those that are store-bought, and those the child improvises for himself. Generally speaking, store-bought toys are fairly worthless for this age child. They tend to be one-dimensional—capable, in other words, of being one thing, and one thing only. A truck is a truck is a truck. A whatever is a whatever is a whatever. As such, store-bought whatevers offer a child little opportunity for truly creative, improvisational play.

Creative toys are capable of being more than one thing. The more things the toy is capable of becoming, the more creative the toy. In this category, we find such store-bought toys as blocks, Lego construction bricks, Tinker Toys, Lincoln Logs, crayons, and finger paints. Notice that all the aforementioned toys were in production before 1955. Since then, very few toys of creative value have been produced. Creative toys also include such everyday things as empty boxes, wooden spoons, pots and pans, empty oatmeal containers, thread spools, pieces of scrap wood, string, and Mom's and Dad's old clothes. In general, a toddler will be more content playing with any of these things than a piece of expensive injection-molded plastic.

These sorts of playthings help a child get in touch with what I call the "Magical Make-Do of Childhood." Making do is the essence of resourcefulness, which is the essence of creativity. Making do is the ability to do a lot with a little. Making do is when you want to make a forest, you go outside and gather pinecones. Each pinecone becomes a pine tree. Making do is when you want to put a house in the middle of your forest of pine cones, you use a shoe box. Making do is when you want furniture for your shoe box house in your pinecone forest, you use spools and stones and smaller boxes and bottle caps and other fancy stuff.

A child doesn't learn to do a lot with a little if his parents gift him with a lot of store-bought toys. Too many toys overwhelm a child's ability to choose a plaything and keep himself occupied. Too many toys prevent the emergence of imaginative play. Too many toys make it all but impossible for a child to learn to make do. Invariably, children who complain a great deal of being "bored," of "having nothing to do," are children who have been given too much. They can simply make no creative sense of the clutter of toys in their environments.

"Yes," you say, "I'd love for my child to have nothing but empty boxes and the like to play with, but his grandparents buy him thing after thing after thing. What am I to do?"

I have the solution to the "grandparent problem," one that's not likely to make anyone upset. Tell these doting grandparents you think it's wonderful they want to do so much for their grandchild. But you think it best they kept the toys they buy at their house. That way, you see, your child always knows that certain toys are gifts from his grandparents. That way, the toys become more special, the grandparents become more special, and going to their house becomes more of a special adventure! Hey, who can argue with that?

I know, your child's grandparents, right? In that case, as soon as they leave, spirit the toys away. Bring them out of hiding five minutes before their next visit.

Effective Communication

Where there is a two-year-old, there is a parent who's asking, "Is there some key, some secret, to getting this child to do what I tell him to do?" Actually, it's more a plea than a question. There's a sense of urgency, of desperation, in the parent's tone and body language, a hint of imminent lunacy in the eyes.

Twos are definitely a breed unto themselves, and the honest answer to the question is, "No, there is not *one* key that will reliably turn the lock of obedience with this age child." But neither is there cause for despair, for there are means of, if not guaranteeing, then surely improving one's chances of getting cooperation.

Environmental management goes a long way toward reducing disciplinary problems, but not, in most cases, far enough. The healthiest of home environments doesn't guarantee cooperation. You take your second of three steps toward disciplinary nirvana by employing the "Three C's of Effective Communication"—Be *Clear, Concise,* and *Commanding.*

Clarity is achieved by speaking concretely, specifically. Don't say, for example, something like, "Mommy wants you to be a good boy while we're in the store, okay?" Instead, tell your little bull in the china shop of life exactly what you want him to do while in the store, and keep it simple. Don't rattle off a list of ten, or even three, dos and don'ts. How about one? Try, "While we're in the store, you must stay in your stroller. Got it?"

"But," you might say, "I want him to keep his hands off things and not throw tantrums and be quiet while I'm talking to salespersons and not spit at people who stop to say 'hello' to him and . . ."

Yes, I know you want him to do and not do all of those things, but he's only two. He can't remember all that. As a consequence, he will not cooperate in any of it. Expect him to remember just one thing, the most important thing, and "cut your losses" concerning the rest.

Clarity also means not using the word "don't." Two-year-olds have difficulty understanding exactly what "don't" means. When you say, "Don't climb on the table," your two-year-old hears, "Gibberish climb on the table." So, he climbs on the table. You might instead simply say "No!" (not yelled, but with emphasis) and quickly remove him from the table. Or, just "Get down!"

You may have already figured out that to be clear you must also be concise. Don't use fifty words when five will do. Besides, with this age child, if five won't do, then no amount will. Being concise also means not explaining yourself. Twos understand simple instructions, but not explanations. Going back to the previous example, a two-year-old who's climbing on a table will understand a firm "Get down," but will not understand "Sweetie, you need to get down from the table because you could fall and hurt yourself and we might have to take you to the doctor and that would make Mommy sad because I don't like to see my little boy get hurt, okay?"

In this case, the child will only hear "Gibberish table, gibberish fall, more gibberish doctor, blah, blah, Mommy, goombah hurt." He'll translate: The table fell on the doctor and Mommy got hurt. So, do yourself and your child a favor and keep it to "Get down."

This brings us to the third of our three C's: commanding. To command is the opposite of being wishy-washy. You are wishy-washy when you plead, bargain, bribe, or threaten. Yes, even threaten, because every threat, in the final analysis, is empty. You are commanding when you preface what you want with either "I want . . ." or "You must . . ." or "It's time for you to. . ." or something equally assertive. So, instead of saying either "If you'll pick up these toys, I'll give you ice cream," or "If you don't pick up these toys, I'll rip you limb from limb," say "It's time for you to pick up your toys."

Ha, ha, ha. I must be kidding, right? You say, "It's time et cetera," and the wily one just stands there and looks at you as if to say, "Make me." What next?

Next you wait for a *strategic opportunity*. In other words, instead of launching yourself impulsively into battle with your child, you leave the toys where they are, bide your time, and wait until your child wants something from you. Twenty minutes later, for instance, he asks you to read him a story. You take his hand, lead him over to the toys, and say, "Before Mommy can read you a story, you must pick up these toys." And he does. Maybe. Please keep in mind that there are no perfect solutions, just potential solutions that are better than others.

But I jump ahead of myself, because waiting for a strategic opportunity is but one example of *proactive* or *managerial* discipline, which we shall take up forthwith, as in right now.

Proactivity

One of the most unfortunate of prevailing attitudes toward disciplining children is the emphasis placed on punishment. When a child misbehaves, parents aren't likely to ask, "What is the most appropriate response?" Instead, the probable question is, "How should we punish?"

The idea that when a child misbehaves, he or she should be punished in some discomforting manner is rooted in our Judeo-Christian consciousness. The most popular of all discomforting punishments is spanking. Although it began falling out of favor in the '60s and early '70s, spanking has recently been endorsed by several child-rearing "experts." But proponents of the "if you can't entreat 'em, beat 'em" school of discipline are sadly mistaken. The key to effective discipline is not punishment, but management.

A managerial approach to discipline offers parents far more options than does a punitive one. Of the two, management is more flexible and creative. As such, it brings out the creative best in a parent.

Punishment is reactive. More often than not, it's a knee-jerk response to having the proverbial rug jerked out from underneath and, for that reason, is usually driven by a certain amount of frustration and/or anger. Management, on the other hand, is *proactive.* Its success depends upon foresight and planning. And preparedness, as every Boy Scout knows, is the best way of keeping frustration under control.

Punishment is confrontational. The inevitable outcome is either win-lose or lose-lose, either of which is undesirable in the parent-child relationship. Ironically, whereas punishment may temporarily suppress a power struggle, it almost always sets the stage for a later one. In no time at all, parent and child become engaged in a vicious, circular game of who can outmaneuver the other.

It's difficult, if not impossible, for a halfway sensitive parent to deliver punishment without feeling some measure of regret afterward. No one likes to feel bad, especially about themselves, so *parents who punish are understandably inconsistent.* Inconsistency prevents a child from being able to anticipate the consequences of his or her behavior and make appropriate adjustments. A punitive approach to discipline, therefore, not only promotes and prolongs testing, but also prevents a child from learning self-control. As such, it is incompatible with the overall aim of discipline. *Punishment alone often creates the illusion that the "crime" has been paid for, that the child has no further debt.* Take, for example, a child who talks back to another adult and whose parents punish by spanking and keeping him indoors for the remainder of the day. While that may deter future disrespect, it fails to make the child accept full responsibility for his or her actions. A sound managerial approach would involve having the child make an unassisted apology to the offended adult.

To be sure, there are times when a child should "pay a price" for misbehavior. But *because of its negative flavor, a constant diet of punitive discipline can eventually damage a child's self-concept.* A properly executed managerial approach to discipline, on the other hand, assists a child toward learning how to successfully manage himself, socially and emotionally. Self-discipline is intrinsically rewarding. As such, a managerial approach to discipline is consistent with a child's need for a positive self-concept.

Proactivity is the primary, defining characteristic of a strategic, managerial approach to discipline. I refer to it as "striking while the iron is cold." This simply means that the most effective time for dealing with misbehavior is *before* it occurs.

Most of us have heard the expression, "strike while the iron is *hot.*" It means you should seize opportunity when it's first presented. It's another way of saying that in hesitation, all may be lost. Although striking while the iron is hot may apply well to certain situations, it does not apply well to the discipline of children. In fact, many valuable teaching opportunities are lost because parents tend to strike at disciplinary situations *only* when the iron is hot.

I am referring to cases in which a child misbehaves and parents react punitively, in anger and frustration. Within the framework of this sort of knee-jerk, *reactive* approach to discipline, the intended lesson is lost in a cacophony of emotion. Because parents inadvertently fail to communicate their expectations clearly, the child continues making the same behavioral mistakes. Proactive discipline, on the other hand, all but ensures that parents will respond with confidence and balance to behavior problems. Because their emotions are in check, the parents are able to communicate clearly, and the child is able to listen.

Proactive discipline is a four-step process:

• First, you *accept* that a certain problem is likely to occur in a certain situation. You *anticipate* the problem, based on either a knowledge of your child or children in general.

• Next comes the *planning* stage, during which you develop a strategy for dealing with the problem. There are, by the way, relatively few *wrong* strategies. In the final analysis, what you do about a problem is less important than knowing what you are going to do *before* the problem occurs.

• Having developed your plan of action, you then *communicate* your proactive decision to the child. You define the problem and describe your strategy. With a two-year-old, remember the importance of being concise, as in, "Today, if you run away from me in the park, I'm going to take you home."

• Finally when the problem occurs, you implement your strategy, following through as often as necessary until the problem is resolved.

Parents often ask me for the secret of keeping one's cool when children misbehave. The secret is proactivity, not some effort of personality. In being proactive, remember that you accept the inevitability of the problem. If you accept the problem is likely to occur, what is there to get angry about when it does? Furthermore, when it occurs, you already know what you're going to do about it. Proactive discipline, therefore, all but ensures that when behavior problems arise, you will be able to respond with both feet planted firmly on the ground.

If you fail to be proactive, then when disciplinary problems arise you will feel yourself being thrown off balance. As a result, you will react emotionally and, therefore, ineffectively.

For example, let's say you don't have any choice but to take your two-and-a-half-year-old along on a shopping trip. You know from experience that a tantrum is likely to occur in the store. You take a few moments to consider your options and decide what you're going to do when the all-but-inevitable tantrum begins.

In this case, you decide simply to take your child back to the car until the tantrum subsides. (I should mention, at this point, that with this age child, it's not always necessary that you *communicate* your strategy beforehand.) When the tantrum begins, you simply pick your child up (holding him facing away from you, of course), saying, "I won't let you scream in stores. We're going to the car where you can scream all you want." And to the car you go.

By anticipating and planning for it, the tantrum doesn't take you by surprise. Because you don't feel upended, you are able to communicate a sense of confidence, of authority, to your child. As a result, your child is able to regain his own balance more quickly. Sound too good to be true? Try it, and discover for yourself.

In this age of stimulus-response psychology, one of the biggest words in the vocabulary of discipline is *consequences.* When a child misbehaves, people tend to think in terms of doing something to persuade the child that the misbehavior in question will not result in what's called a *payoff.* Consequences certainly have their place, but the emphasis put on them has blinded many people to other, equally effective means of dealing with behavior problems. Sometimes, consequences aren't necessary at all. Sometimes, as the following story illustrates, *cunning* is all it takes:

Several years ago, my wife and I were having lunch with our two-year-old godson, Travis, and his mother. Travis dropped his napkin on the floor, and his mother told him to pick it up. He gave her "the look" and did nothing. She told him again, more insistently. Travis just sat there. Finally, she gave up.

A few minutes later, Travis heard an airplane flying overhead and became very excited. I said, "Would you like to fly airplanes someday, Travis?" He nodded his head enthusiastically, and so I followed up with, "Then you have to pick up your napkin." He promptly got down and picked up the napkin.

Just another example of waiting for a *strategic opportunity.* Put another way, good things come to those who wait.

Consistency

Unless parents are consistent with their discipline, a child cannot predict consequences. A child's ability to predict consequences and adjust behavior accordingly is the essence of self-discipline. It follows, therefore, that a child cannot learn to discipline himself unless his parents first discipline him with consistency.

Any child can be counted upon to test any rule. Testing is a child's only way of discovering whether, in fact, the rule truly exists. Telling the child "This is a rule" isn't convincing enough. Children—especially young ones—are concrete thinkers. Rules must be *demonstrated*. So, when a child breaks a rule, parents have an obligation to impose some form of discipline. This gets the child's attention and says, "See? We were telling you the truth." So, parents demonstrate their reliability by being consistent. The more a child knows he can rely upon his parents, the more secure the child will feel.

If, on the other hand, a child breaks a stated rule, and instead of *doing something assertive*, parents threaten or talk themselves blue in the face or get excited but don't do anything, the child is forced to test the rule again. And again. And again. Testing of this sort "spins the child's wheels." It wastes time and energy the child could otherwise use in creative, constructive activity. Consistency frees children from the burden of having to test rules repeatedly. Therefore, consistency helps children become all they are capable of becoming.

Many parents think that being consistent means administering the same discipline each and every time a child misbehaves in a certain manner. Not so. Consistency is more a matter of attitude than technique. In fact, it is unrealistic to suppose that you will always be able to deliver the same technique every time a child misbehaves in a certain way. But you can always deliver the same *attitude*. In other words, you can display your disapproval and do something as a demonstration that you are in control. The something you do doesn't have to be the same something from misbehavior to misbehavior. It just needs to be something that says, "I won't allow you to behave like that."

Say your two-year-old becomes disruptive while you have company. You take him to his crib and leave the room. He screams and shakes the sides of the crib for a minute or two. You go back to his room and, standing in his doorway, ask, "Are you ready to come out and play quietly with your toys?" He says he is, but still may need to test you a few more times before he's convinced you mean business.

The next day, he becomes disruptive in a restaurant. You take him outside, explaining to the manager as you go that you'll be back to finish your meal as soon as your young'n quiets down. You take your "terrible" two-year-old to the car, put him in his car seat, and get in the front seat. You then say, "When you stop screaming, we'll go back in the restaurant and finish our food." A minute later, he's still screaming. You turn around and say, "Are you ready to go back in and finish your lunch?" He says he is, but still may need to test you a time or two before he's convinced you mean business.

You handled his disruptions at home and his disruptions in the restaurant differently, yet similarly enough. You were, therefore, consistent from one situation to the next. Perhaps he becomes disruptive in a store a week hence. You had planned on buying him a new pair of shoes, but you say, "No shoes today," and take him home. He gets the message: You do not allow loud, attention-seeking behavior. Because of your consistency, he is eventually able to predict that when he is loud, you are going to do something that won't be to his liking. He doesn't, however, know exactly *what* you're going to do. But that's not important. What's important is he knows you're going to do *something*. As a result, he begins exercising more control over himself. He learns to discipline himself. And that's what parental discipline is all about!

Containment vs. Correction

Before we go any further, and before you get the feeling I'm leading you down the proverbial primrose path, I need to tell you that it's not always possible to *correct* the behavior of a two-year-old. In other words, if your toddler has developed a certain undesirable behavior, you may just have to live with it till he's at least three. During this time you may have to accept that the behavior in question can only be *contained*. The good news is that a misbehavior that is properly contained is a misbehavior that, when the time comes, can be easily corrected.

Two-year-olds are impulsive. They don't think ahead, and they don't have much hindsight, either. As a result, it takes a great deal of persistence to get disciplinary messages across to them. For example, let's say your two-year-old refuses to take a nap. You not only think he needs a nap, but *you* need him to take a nap. He also refuses to stay in his bed at night, and putting him back in a crib isn't the answer, because he can climb out of his crib. You've tried spanking him, but that only made him that much more determined (as spankings often do with this age child). You've told him that if he doesn't stay in his room at nap time, you won't take him outside later. He doesn't seem to care. You've tried reasoning with him, explaining the benefits of sleep. Ha! Now what?

Now you must accept that you aren't going to be able to correct this problem until he's older. For now, you can only contain it. So, you hire a carpenter to cut your son's bedroom door in half. He rehangs the two halves, making a "Dutch" door, and turns the lock around on the bottom half. Now, when you put your son in for a nap, you close the bottom half of his new door and lock it. He can't get out, but he can still see out.

The first few times you do this, he screams bloody murder. He's not afraid, mind you, just mad as hell. Each time, you wait a few minutes before going back to his room. You peer over the bottom half of his door and say, "Everything's all right. I'm in the living room reading a book. It's time for you to get into your bed and take a nap. I'm going back to the living room now." You walk away. He continues to scream. You wait a few minutes and do the same thing, and you keep going back to his room every few minutes until he's quiet, which may take an hour or more the first time you do this.

Does it matter whether he actually takes a nap? No. What matters is that he stays in his room for an hour or so, giving you some time to yourself. Eventually, he accepts being put in his room at nap time, accepts the fact he can't get out, and plays for ninety minutes. You haven't corrected the problem, but you've contained it. You've established boundaries around the problem, limiting it to manageable proportions. When he's three, you can tell him that if he comes out of his room before nap time is over, you won't take him outside later. At three, he can think ahead. So, he listens and stays in his room. Now you can buy a new door.

The difference between correction and containment applies to many problems typical to the stage of development under discussion. At this age, for example, tantrums are all but impossible to eliminate, but they can be contained. When our daughter, Amy, was two, she began throwing wild tantrums over anything and everything that didn't go her way. We tried the usual approaches: spanking her and ignoring her. Neither worked. Finally, we came to our senses and realized we were fighting a losing battle. She wan't going to stop throwing tantrums until she had developed a better tolerance for frustration. Until then, we could only contain her fits of pique. So, we child-proofed the downstairs bathroom and presented it to her as her new "tantrum place."

"From now on, Amy," we told her, "every time you want to have a tantrum, we're going to put you in this special tantrum place, and you can have your tantrum here. We picked the bathroom because it has a carpet for you to roll around on, and if you scream so loudly that you have to go to the bathroom, you're already there!"

From that time on, every time Amy began to scream when things didn't go her way, we simply said, "You can only throw tantrums in your tantrum place, Amy," and took her to the bathroom as quickly as we could. As soon as we closed the door, she'd stop screaming. Nonetheless, she'd stay in there for a few minutes—fuming, we supposed—before emerging. Did this stop her from having tantrums? No, it only contained them to a certain area of the house. She continued to throw them until she was three, when they began tapering off.

The point I'm trying to make is that if you try to eliminate an undesirable behavior with this age child, you may only frustrate yourself. Concentrate instead on containing the behavior. Containment may be all that's realistically possible. In addition, the assertiveness and self-control you display in the course of containing the behavior will pay off in spades when your child is old enough for you to begin actually "correcting."

Setting Disciplinary Precedents

The disciplinary style you develop when your child is this age will be precedent-setting. It's important, therefore, that the precedents you set be of long-term benefit to both you and your child. In all that I've said in this chapter, and in all I've yet to say, I'm trying to illustrate a disciplinary style that embodies the following elements:

- Management, as opposed to punishment.
- Proactivity, as opposed to reactivity.
- Assertiveness, as opposed to anger.
- Consistency, as opposed to unpredictability.
- Communication, as opposed to confusion.

If you succeed at incorporating these characteristics into your discipline at this stage of the game, then discipline should never be a "big deal" in your relationship with your child. Why? Because a disciplinary style that embodies these elements is a disciplinary style that fosters self-discipline. And the earlier, and better, your child disciplines himself, the more of a joy your parenthood will be.

I once counseled a family in which the "problem child" was a sixteen-year-old whom we shall call Lynnette. Over the two years prior to my seeing the family, Lynnette had become extremely rebellious. She took every possible opportunity to "sneak around," as her parents put it. She associated with kids her parents disapproved of, went places her parents told her she was not to go, and did things her parents forbade, like drinking and smoking.

One of the stories her parents told was especially interesting: Almost every time Lynnette would go somewhere in the family car, she would bring it back with empty beer cans in the back seat or half-smoked marijuana cigarettes in the ashtray. It was as if she was flaunting her disregard of her parents' rules. When her parents confronted her with the "evidence," however, Lynnette would deny knowing anything about it. She'd claim that one of her friends must have put the beer cans in the back seat without her knowledge, that someone to whom she gave a ride must have left the "joint" in the ashtray. Her parents could never get her to admit to any wrongdoing.

One day, her parents saw me in an especially frustrated state of mind. At one point during the visit, her mother said, "I knew when Lynnette was two that she was going to be a permanent headache."

"How's that?" I asked.

Her mother told me that when Lynnette was two, she would hold her bowel movements by squeezing her legs together. When asked if she had to go to the bathroom, she would insist that she didn't. Later, her parents would find a bowel movement in a corner of the living room or, even worse, in a shoebox in the parents' bedroom closet.

"I'd ask her if she had made the b.m.," her mother said, "and she'd always deny it. I could never get her to admit that she was the one who'd pooped in the corner or in the shoebox."

I immediately realized that the precedent her parents had set when Lynnette was two years old was still operating in their relationship. At two, she pooped in the corner and denied it. At sixteen, she (figuratively speaking, of course) "pooped" in the family car and denied it. Things hadn't changed in fourteen years.

I've made the same observation time and time again in the course of counseling families. For better or worse, the themes that characterize the parent-child relationship when the child is two are the same themes that characterize the relationship later, especially during the child's early and middle teen years. A relatively smooth relationship at two predicts a relatively smooth relationship at fourteen. On the other hand, a rocky relationship at two predicts likewise at fourteen.

So, get it together now, and you may never have to get it together again!

Biting Off What You Can Chew

Good discipline doesn't have to be complicated. Rather, it must be well organized, easily communicated, and easily dispensed. The simpler, the better. Nothing will kill a discipline plan quicker than weighing it down with dozens of unnecessary "if-then" considerations, as in: If you clean your room, you get a star. If you don't, you get a check. At the end of the week, we subtract checks from stars and give you a quarter for each "point" that results. If there are more checks than stars, you owe us money, which we take off the top of next week's allowance. If there are no checks, you get a bonus. If, however, you were "in the hole" before the week started, the bonus is applied to the debt.

See what I mean? Much too complicated.

Another way of dooming discipline to failure is to bite off more than you can chew. Let's take, for example, a child who's destructive, disobedient, irresponsible, unmotivated, aggressive, disrespectful, and loud. Instead of tackling all the problems at once, which would be like wrestling with an octopus, it would be better to concentrate on just one—the easiest one. Solving one problem puts you in a good position to solve another, and then another, and so on.

The parents of two children, ages five and two, were having the usual problems that come with having two young'ns. They sassed, squabbled, screamed, jumped on furniture, wrote on the walls, ran through the house, got into everything, and created general bedlam. The parents raced from one child to the other, one thing to the next, driving themselves bananas in the process. They reminded me of the plate-spinners I used to see on the "Ed Sullivan Show." The more they tried to accomplish, the less they accomplished.

"Pick three problems," I told them.

They picked sassing, squabbling, and screaming. Neither child could read, so we drew pictures, one for each problem. Screaming was represented by a stick-child with mouth wide open; squabbling by two stick-children yelling at one another; sassing by a stick-child sticking a stick-tongue out at a stick-parent. Artists, we weren't.

The pictures were posted on the refrigerator and the children were told what each of them meant. The parents bought a timer and kept it handy to the children's rooms. When one of the targeted behaviors occurred, the parent closest at hand would identify the behavior ("That's sassing") and say, "That's one of your pictures and means you have to spend ten minutes in your room(s)." The parent would take the offending child or children to his/her/their room(s), set the timer for ten minutes, and walk away. When the bell rang, the children could come out of their neutral corners.

I stressed the importance of adhering to what I call "the referee's rule": No threats, no second chances, no deals. "When an infraction occurs," I said, speaking figuratively, "blow the whistle and assess the penalty. And remember that in hesitation, indecision, or negotiation, all is lost."

I saw them again three weeks later. Mom started off by telling me she had finally found a whistle at a sporting goods store. I was incredulous.

"You mean you actually went out and bought a real referee's whistle?"

"Sure did," Mom replied. "It sounded like a good idea to me. When we're home, I wear it around my neck. When I blow the whistle, the kids march to their rooms. I don't even have to tell them to go. Better yet, they've learned to set the timer themselves."

I asked how she felt about the plan, and here's what she told me, word for word: "I feel more confident in my parenting skills, and more in control of my children. The children are reacting in a way that tells me they're more confident of my authority. They've learned my limits. Before, we were at the point of constant frenzy. Now the household is calm. It's a very organized feeling, and everyone is happier!"

Strike another blow for simplicity.

Those Four Bad Words

My first book in this series, *John Rosemond's Six-Point Plan for Raising Happy, Healthy Children*, hadn't been out four weeks when I received a letter from a reader in Albuquerque chastising me for giving parents permission to say "because I said so." She was upset because when she was a child, "because I said so" was her parents' answer to everything. "Children need to know the reasons behind the decisions parents make," she wrote.

I agree that many of our parents used "because I said so" simply to get us to shut up. The implied threat was that if we didn't bite our tongues, serious consequences would be forthcoming. But whereas those four words may at times convey a rigid, unreasonable attitude, they are not, in and of themselves, unreasonable.

The primary function of being a parent is that of acquainting children with reality. Part of that reality is that, even in a democratic society, authority figures—teachers, lawmakers, employers—frequently impose arbitrary decisions. Someone in authority decides things are going to be done one way as opposed to another, and that's the way they are done. Why? Because an authority figure said so. And the rest of us have to live with it.

By my estimation, approximately four of every five parental decisions are founded on nothing more substantial than personal preference. When that's the case, some variation on "because I said so" is the most honest answer to a child's demand to know "Why?" Unfortunately, partly because those four words were crammed down many of our throats as children and partly because the "experts" arbitrarily decided that "because I said so" was harmful to children, many of today's parents feel they don't have permission to say it.

By and large, today's parents feel they are obligated to explain themselves to their children. Furthermore, they seem to believe that their explanations must be acceptable to their children. Consequently, their explanations take on a persuasive, pleading, even apologetic character. Implicit in this is the absolutely absurd idea that parents don't have a right to enforce a decision unless (a) it can be supported by reasons other than personal preference, (b) the children understand the reasons, and (c) the children agree with them.

Now, hear me clearly: *I'm not saying that parents should never give reasons to children.* I'm saying parents should make no attempt to *reason with* children, and the difference is night and day. Reasoning is the futile attempt to persuade a child that your point of view is valid. Face it, our children will understand an adult point of view when they are adults, and no sooner. No amount of words will instill an appreciation for an adult point of view into the mind of a child.

If you want to explain yourself, then by all means do so. But don't expect your child to agree. When he doesn't, simply say, "I'm not asking you to agree. I wouldn't agree with me, either, if I was your age. You have my permission to disagree, but you don't have permission to disobey."

In other words, the child does what he is told not because you succeed at providing an explanation that smooths his ruffled feathers, but simply because he's been told. So, you see, even in the act of giving reasons, the bottom line is still "because I said so."

Not Mean Enough

"I feel so mean," said the mother of a boisterous and very strong-willed three-year-old girl. "I yell all the time," she said.

"Yelling isn't mean," I said.

Her expression changed to bewilderment, and she stared at me for several seconds before asking, "What is it, then?"

"It's not anything but yelling, and yelling is nothing. As you've already discovered, yelling accomplishes nothing, unless you consider the guilt you feel afterward an accomplishment. Your problem is not that you are too mean, it's that you aren't mean enough."

After another bewildered look, she said, "Not mean enough?"

"Right!" I said. "Not mean enough. In order to accomplish what you want to accomplish with this very headstrong and active little girl of yours, you're going to have to get truly mean."

"I'm afraid I'm lost."

"Let me explain. Mean isn't screaming and yelling. That's out of control. Mean isn't cruel, either. Truly *mean* parents are calm, consistent, and insistent. They do not tolerate misbehavior, although they know it's bound to occur. Knowing it's inevitable, they don't get angry when it happens.

"Mean parents are assertive. They don't give second, third, and fourth chances. They insist that children do what they're told, the first time they're told. They don't count to ten or engage in other equally ridiculous games of chance. They don't make threats, they make promises. Meanest of all, they *keep* their promises.

"Mean parents are consistent. They uphold the same standards from one day to the next. The ways they enforce those standards may vary from situation to situation, but the standards themselves do not. Their children, therefore, can rely upon them. They learn to trust that what their parents say is exactly what their parents are going to do.

"Mean parents don't shoulder emotional responsibility for their children's misbehavior. When the child of truly mean parents misbehaves, the parents don't feel bad about it. Instead, they make sure the *child* feels bad about it. Mean parents don't run interference for their children, either. They don't make excuses for their kids and they let them make mistakes. They allow them the benefits of learning by trial and error, with emphasis on the *error.*

"It's very simple, really. Mean parents make rules and enforce them dispassionately, without any great to-do. Their children may not like the rules, but they respect them."

"But," she said, "my daughter already accuses me of being mean."

"Your daughter doesn't know what she's talking about. She uses the word *mean* simply because she's learned it jerks the rug out from underneath you. When she calls you 'mean,' you get upset, you feel guilty, you start backtracking, explaining yourself, apologizing, and maybe even giving in. She says you're 'mean,' and you feel like a bad parent. But to a truly mean parent, being called 'mean' is the highest of compliments."

"But don't children grow up to resent you if you're mean?" she asked.

"There you go, confusing mean with nasty. Mean parents create a loving climate characterized by certainty and security and trust. What is there to resent?"

"It sounds like being mean is really in a child's best interest."

"You've got it! Now, go do it!"

Hair Today, Gone Tomorrow

Caroline was twenty-one months old. Like most children her age, she liked to rummage through and around and in and out of places and things like drawers and cabinets and boxes of cereal her mother left out on the table for Caroline to find and dump on the floor.

Unlike most children her age, however, Caroline pulled her hair out. Twist and yank and the deed was done. Then, back to rummaging she would go. As far as Caroline was concerned, yanking out strands of hair was just something you did, like climbing on the table and dumping out cereal boxes.

When Caroline first started yanking out her hair, around age eighteen months, her parents responded with relatively low levels of concern. They talked to her about her pretty hair and told her not to pull any more of it out. And so, she pulled more of it out.

Her parents' concern soon turned to worry. They talked more and more about her pretty hair and how it should stay in her head and began speaking sharply to her and slapping her hand when they caught her twisting. The more they worried and talked and reprimanded, the more hair Caroline yanked. Finally, bald spots were appearing all over her head. She began bringing hair by the palmfuls to her parents and proudly announcing, "Hair!"

I saw all three of them in my office. Caroline played on the floor while her parents and I talked.

"What's wrong with Caroline?" they asked.

"Nothing that I can tell," I replied.

"Why, then, does she pull her hair out?"

"Do either of you bite your fingernails?" I asked. They admitted they both did.

"What's the difference?" I asked.

"Well," said Caroline's mother, "my fingernails will grow back."

"So will Caroline's hair," I pointed out.

"But why is she pulling it out in the first place?" they demanded to know.

"It probably first occurred by accident," I answered. "She just happened to do it once in the normal course of rummaging over herself. She continued to do it because you started acting like it was the most important thing in the whole world. How's Caroline to know? She even began bringing you gifts of hair, thinking it would please you."

"Should we ignore it, then?" her father asked.

"No," I answered, "because you can't, and to tell you the truth, neither could I. Here's my idea: The next time Caroline brings you a gob of hair, take her by the hand, lead her into the bathroom and show her how to flush it down the toilet. Then walk away without saying another word. From that point on, every time she brings you hair, just tell her to go flush it. If you find gobs on the floor, tell her to flush them, too."

Caroline's parents did exactly that, and within a month, Caroline's bald spots were beginning to fill in. Nothing was ever wrong with Caroline. She just got temporarily distracted from her rummaging.

Questions?

Q *Several weeks ago, our eighteen-month-old son had a bowel movement while we were giving him a bath. Needless to say, we were all somewhat surprised, but Josh was downright frightened. Since then, when it comes time for his bath, he climbs into the tub, but refuses to sit down. If we attempt to force him, he stiffens and goes into hysterics. Several times, he has promised us he's going to sit, but once in the tub, he changes his mind.*

We've also talked reassuringly about the "accident." The talks go fine, but nothing changes. This may not sound like a big problem, but it's got us at wit's end. Do you have any suggestions?

A Sounds like your typical toddler-parent standoff—he won't sit for it, and you won't stand for it.

Let's review the situation: Josh is in the tub splashing water all over everyone, blowing bubbles, giggling, when suddenly . . . What's this? . . . Oh, my goodness, Dr. Spock never told us this would happen. Josh doesn't understand what's going on, but he can tell by the looks on your faces that whatever it is, it isn't good. So he moves fast to get out, and you move fast to get him out. The next time you announce a bath, Josh faces a dilemma. He likes the tub, but he doesn't like what happened the last time he was there, and he's sure as heck not going to put himself in that same position again.

"I'll just stand, thank you."

"No, you'll sit."

"No, I'll stand!"

"Sit!"

"Stand!"

Haven't you heard? Toddlers have minds of their own. Strong ones, too. In fact, extensive laboratory research has determined that the mind of the average toddler is stronger by 1.5 quantities than the average adult biceps, so the more you pull, the more-and-a-half Josh pushes. Meanwhile, the issue gets big, then bigger, then biggest. The bigger the issue, the stronger his will, and the weaker, by comparison, your bicep.

Forget reasoning with Josh. He's on to your tricks. The fancy words, the soothing tone, all designed to lull him into a sense of false security. Josh (to himself): "They think I'm dumb. Watch this."

Parents: "Josh, listen, the other day you pooped in the tub and blah, blah, blah, it was just an accident and blah, blah, blah, it's dangerous to stand and blah, blah, and furthermore blah, blah, you understand, don't you, sweetheart?"

Josh (nodding convincingly): Uh-huh."

Parents: "Good! Then sit down."

Josh: "Nope. Stand."

Nice try, folks. Back to the drawing board. Instead of trying to meet Josh's willpower head on, instead of trying to convince him there's nothing to worry about, offer him a "strategic compromise." That's where you get him to do what you want, but make it seem like it was all his idea. It's rumored that wives often do this with their husbands.

A "strategic compromise" is parent-judo. In this case, you need to make Josh an offer that appears to compromise your position, but doesn't compromise either your authority or Josh's autonomy. It's easier than it may sound.

Being proactive, before Josh's next bath, you say, "Josh, you don't have to sit in the tub tonight, but you can't stand, either, because you might fall down. So, you have to kneel, like this."

Demonstrate what you're talking about and have him practice a few times, praising him for his excellent kneeling. Once he's mastered the technique, take him to the tub.

Now you've got him. Once Josh experiences the "joys" of kneeling, he's going to want to find a more comfortable position. But you told him he can't stand, so what's left? You've got it! Problem solved!

Q *Over the last few months, our twenty-month-old son has developed the disturbing habit of violently banging his head on a hard surface, like the floor, when he's frustrated. I've tried teaching him alternative ways of expressing his feelings, such as foot stomping, but with no success. As a result, he has a constantly bruised forehead. A child psychologist I talked with told me to ignore it, but I'm afraid Sam will hurt himself if I do. When he starts banging I stop him, at which point he struggles with me. This happens several times a day. Other than this, Sam's a cheerful little guy. I believe this is a phase, but I was hoping you might have a way of bringing it to a quick end.*

A You're absolutely right. Sam will eventually stop banging his head. But if you do the right thing, he'll stop sooner than he would have otherwise. Contrary to the psychologist's advice, ignoring it is the wrong thing to do. Not only will

Sam's head banging not go away if you ignore it, but it causes you too much anxiety to ignore. Besides, he could conceivably cause himself serious injury if you don't put some limits on the behavior.

Before we go any further let's get one thing straight: You can no more prevent him from banging his head than you can prevent him from throwing a tantrum. If he wants to throw a tantrum he's going to, and if he wants to bang his head he's going to. Toddlers have a reputation for reacting to frustration by doing bizarre things like banging their heads, biting themselves, and pulling out their hair—the kinds of aberrant behavior we associate with the inmates of an eighteenth-century insane asylum. No need to worry, however, for it's all normal to the age. Toddlers bang their heads and bite themselves and throw themselves around because they're uncivilized. They continue to do things of this sort because of the attention these behaviors bring. The trick, then, is to come up with a way of not giving Sam attention for head banging without, however, ignoring it.

There's a way of doing just that. It's a bit out of the ordinary, but I've recommended it successfully a number of times, so I know it works. First, find a section of blank wall in some relatively out-of-the-way, yet accessible, part of the house. Using a washable crayon, draw a two-foot diameter circle on the wall, positioning the center at the height of Sam's forehead. Make sure that any wall studs are off to the side of the circle, rather than dead center. Show Sam the circle and tell him that this is his very own head-banging place. Whenever he wants to bang his head, he should come here and bang because this is the best place in the whole world for that kind of thing.

Since you've also been teaching him to stomp his feet, you can draw a circle on the floor, directly beneath the head-banging circle, and tell him it's his very own special foot-stomping place. Now he can bang his head and stomp his foot at the same time, which is bound to help his coordination, if nothing else. Demonstrate how convenient it will be for him to bang his head in the special place by getting down on your knees and banging your own head a few times. Tell him how good it felt and encourage him to give a try.

Yes, I know this sounds strange, but it's kind of like fighting fire with fire. Sam will look at you like you've lost your marbles, and the next time he gets mad he will start banging his head in just any old place. When that happens, pick him up, take him to the special circle. Say, "Bang here in your special place!" and walk away.

If you do this every time he bangs his head, head banging should begin to taper off in a week or so. There's no future in banging your head unless your parents get upset over it. Within a month, it should be a thing of the past. Then he'll probably start biting himself, in which case you draw a circle on his forearm and . . .

Q *I am the besieged parent of a two-year-old. Our pediatrician has recommended that when our daughter misbehaves, we make her sit in a chair for two minutes. It sounds good, but my daughter won't sit there. As soon as I begin to walk away, she gets up and follows me. The doctor told me to train her by setting a timer for two minutes and sitting with her until the bell rings. I tried this for about four weeks and got nowhere. Besides, I had to entertain her for the entire two minutes, which seemed to defeat the purpose of the discipline. Now the pediatrician is telling me to hold her in the chair, which doesn't appeal to me at all. Do you have any ideas?*

A First let me say that I agree with your feelings about sitting with her until the bell rings. I also agree that holding her in the chair for two minutes is not a good idea at all. It will only provoke a struggle and lots of screaming, serving only to replace one problem with another and set the stage for escalating conflict in your relationship.

You can reasonably expect a three-year-old to sit in time-out for two or three minutes, but a younger child, as you've discovered, isn't likely to cooperate in sitting for a specific length of time. The good news, however, is that whether a two-year-old sits or not isn't that important. What's important is that you respond assertively to the problem behavior, whatever it is.

When your daughter misbehaves—say she jumps on the living room sofa—you should first reprimand her ("No jumping!"); second, spell out the consequences ("I'm taking you to the no-no chair."); next, take her to the designated place (it can be any chair in the house, but should be somewhere off by itself) and put her in it while saying, "You're going to sit here until I tell you to get up." Then, take one step back and say, "Okay, you can get up now."

No doubt your daughter will begin getting up as soon as you step back. By giving her immediate permission to get up, you make it appear as if she's cooperating with you. Clever, eh? More important, you'll demonstrate that you are in control of yourself and her as well, and that what you say goes. In the final analysis your *assertiveness* is what counts, not that she cooperates in sitting for a certain length of time.

If you do this consistently, within a couple of weeks your daughter will begin waiting for your signal before getting out of the chair. At that point, you can begin delaying permission to get up until she's sitting for fifteen seconds or so, which is quite long enough for this age child. Teaching her to wait for your signal prepares her for the day when you'll begin using a timer, which you can introduce when she's about three.

Q *I started using the time-out method you recommend with two-year-olds [see the above question-and-answer], and things are already going more smoothly between my thirty-month-old son and myself. He still won't do what he's told, however. I tell him to pick up his toys, and he tells me he's not going to. I put him in the "no-no chair," take several steps away, and tell him he can get up. Then I again tell him to pick up his toys, and he again refuses. Do I put him back in the chair? That could go on all day.*

A Yes, that could go on all day, and no, you wouldn't accomplish anything by putting him back in the "no-no chair" except create a power struggle. No one wins a power struggle. Besides, because of the precedent-setting nature of the stage, power struggles now will only mean more power struggles to come. As I've already pointed out, there are no magic solutions to the disciplinary dilemmas parents encounter with two-year-olds. If a three-year-old won't pick up his toys, you can tell him he's not going outside later. He knows what "later" means, and cares whether he goes outside or not. A two-year-old, on the other hand, couldn't care less about *later.* He only cares about right now, and the important thing right now is he's not going to pick up his toys. So there!

Ah, but if you are patient, a "strategic opportunity" will eventually present itself. Say you want him to pick up his toys, and he refuses. Just shrug your shoulders and walk away, leaving the toys on the floor. Later, when he wants to go outside or wants you to read him a book, take him by the hand, lead him back to the scene of the "crime," and say, "When you pick up these toys I'll take you outside."

At this point, if he's a normal two-year-old, he'll fall on the floor and start thrashing about while screaming at the top of his lungs. Just smile and tell him, "It's okay to scream. When you finish screaming, pick up the toys, and we'll go outside."

Needless to say, two-year-olds are extremely persistent little people. They can hold out for a long, long time. That's why it's important to wait patiently for a suitable strategic opportunity and resolve to hold out even longer. This is a nonpunitive way of asserting your authority that is emotionally cost-effective and keeps you out of power struggles. Once your son realizes you hold the key to the things he wants to do, he'll begin cooperating—most of the time, that is.

Q *Our two-year-old recently decided to become truly "terrible." Is he old enough for us to start spanking him?*

A That depends on what you mean by "spanking," as well as how and when you plan to do it. In my view, a spanking is a spanking only if the following conditions are satisfied:
  • The parent administers the spanking with his or her hand.
  • The parent's hand makes contact with the child's rear end only.
  • The hand strikes the rear no more than twice.

Anything more than described above is a beating. I also recommend that parents spank as a first resort, rather than as "the final straw." The more parents remind and threaten, the more frustrated they become and the more likely it is they will spank in a rage.

Please understand that spankings (as described above) are effective only as a means of either securing a child's attention or terminating a behavior that is rapidly escalating out of control or both. Spankings are not an effective consequence, and should not be used as such. The consequence, whatever it is, should *follow* the spanking, which simply serves to stop the misbehavior and focus the child's attention on the parent.

In and of themselves, spankings do not motivate appropriate behavior. A spanking accompanied by a period of restriction or a brief reprimand will have a much greater positive effect than a spanking alone. Furthermore, children who receive a lot of spankings often become "immune" to them. Therefore, the more conservative parents are about spanking, the more effective each spanking will be.

As a general rule, spankings are not very effective with two-year-olds. In the first place, twos are decidedly determined little people, and spankings often do nothing more than provoke further determination. Furthermore, this age child quickly forgets a spanking. Two minutes later, he's back doing the same thing. A firm but gentle approach to discipline, involving lots of "Grandma's Rule"—the toddler can do what he wants when he's done what *you* want—is far more effective with this age child.

A young child should never be slapped on the back of the hand for touching something off limits. This rule applies even if the child is reaching for something hot. If you have time to slap, then you also have time to grab his hand and pull it away, with a sharp "No!" Now that you have his undivided attention, tell him why he should keep away from the object in question.

During the peak of a child's exploratory period, from eighteen to thirty-six months, it is best and most economical—in terms of time, energy, and even money—simply to remove tempting objects from reach. I've heard parents rationalize their refusal to child-proof by saying, "He's got to learn the difference between what he can and can't touch." Then they follow the toddler around, slapping his hands all day long. Refusing (or being too lazy) to child-proof amounts to nothing more than a weak excuse for refusing to accommodate (and then punishing) the child's need to inquire, explore, discover, and create. It's true there are times when that sequence ends in "destroy." These incidents, however, will be few and far between in a properly child-proofed home. Furthermore, I have found that when parents take the time to patiently teach a child how to handle things gently, the child rarely breaks anything of significance.

Q *Every time—and I mean every single time—I take my thirty-two-month-old son into a store, he quickly finds some reason to create a disturbance or throw a tantrum. I've tried everything from rewards to spankings to get him to behave himself, but nothing has worked. Besides leaving the store and taking him home—which isn't practical because I'd never get any shopping done—do you have any suggestions?*

A I suggest you leave the store and take him home. Bear with me, however, because what I have in mind won't require that you sacrifice your shopping—not much, anyway.

This problem actually presents you with an ideal disciplinary opportunity. With relatively little time and effort, you can not only take positive control of your son's public behavior, but also establish an entirely new disciplinary "tone" in the relationship, one that will take you effectively out of the reward/punishment "rut" in which you're currently stuck.

As it stands, your son begins to misbehave in a store and you *react*. Your response to the problem is, in other words, after the fact and undoubtedly flooded with anger, frustration, and other negative emotions. The elements of reaction and emotion characterize a disciplinary style that's bound to fall flat on its face time after time after time. To turn your son around, you're going to have to first turn yourself around. You need to respond to his behavior *proactively*—before the fact. A proactive response will enable you to remain in control of yourself and your emotions. As a result, your self-confidence—the essence of effective discipline—will shine through.

In this case, the proactive response of choice involves making "dry runs." Plan a trip to the store when you have no shopping to do. On the pretense of having to make a purchase, undertake the excursion as you normally would, taking your son along.

Before you enter the store, however, stop outside and calmly inform your son that should he create a disturbance, no matter how small, you will immediately take him home, where he will spend the remainder of the day indoors with no privileges (television, a friend over) and go to bed early.

Now, instead of dreading a disturbance, you're actually *hoping* for one. When it happens—and it will, believe me—you simply say, "You've just told me that you want to go home, so let's go." Take his hand, lead him immediately out of the store, take him directly home, and do exactly what you said you were going to do. Do not, under any circumstances, give him a second chance or renegotiate the consequence, regardless of what he might promise.

Now you have your son's attention. Instead of getting flustered when he misbehaved, you responded with calm, purposeful resolve. Having taken him by surprise, you can expect a dramatic reaction on his part. He will, in all likelihood, wail and tell you he doesn't want to be your child any longer and then wail some more. Just say, "I'd be upset, too, if I had to go home and spend the rest of the day inside."

Over the next few weeks, plan as many unnecessary excursions to the store as you can, taking the same approach each time. Within a month, your son should be a model shopper. In the meantime, you may have to sacrifice one or two necessary shopping trips as well. If that happens, just remember there's a price to be paid for everything. In this case, however, the payment plan is virtually painless.

Q *My two-year-old son attends a toddler program three mornings a week, and my friend and I take turns carpooling to the center. Last Monday, when she arrived, Iggy suddenly announced he wasn't going with her. When I asked him why not, he screamed,*

"Because I don't want to!" I took him out to the car, but couldn't get him buckled into the seat belt for all his kicking and screaming. After a struggle, I decided to give up and drive him myself. The same thing happened the next two times it was my friend's turn to drive. She suggested I just hand him over and let her handle it, but I don't want to push a screaming two-year-old off on anyone else. I talked to him about it, and he promised to ride with her later, but not now. Can you explain his sudden change in behavior and help me solve this problem?

A Iggy has already told you why he doesn't want to ride with your friend. He doesn't want to! Two-year-olds don't know why they do things. They just decide to do something, then they do it. Why? Because.

You must stop talking so much. You're not going to solve this problem by trying to reason with Iggy. Instead of talking, act! Take charge! If you set the precedent of allowing him to control this situation, then your troubles are just beginning. Take your friend up on her kind offer. If she's willing to put up with Iggy's screaming, take him out to her, hand him over, and walk away. Your friend should put him in her car (if he struggles, she should forget the seat belt), close the door, and drive about fifty yards down the street. She should then pull over and announce to Iggy that he's going to wear his seat belt, just like all the other two-year-olds in the world. She then buckles him in and drives on. I'll bet he'll give her no problem, particularly once you're out of sight.

Oh, I almost forgot something. Just before the next time your friend comes, say this to Iggy: "Guess what, Iggy? So-and-so is coming to take you to school this morning. Remember how you screamed the last time she came? Well, you can scream today, too! It's a fine day for screaming."

When she pulls up and he begins to scream, say, "Good for you! That's a great scream! Let's go out to the car so everyone else can hear you!"

I know, this sounds a bit crazy, but it works, believe me. Several years ago, I gave the same advice to the mother of a toddler who screamed every time she arrived at her morning preschool program. The mother was convinced her child's reluctance to separate from her was indication of some deep-seated insecurity (example of the mischief "helping professionals" have made in the world). I told her simply to encourage her daughter to scream.

So, the next time they were on their way to the program, the mother began saying things like, "This is a fine morning for screaming. You know, when you scream, I know you love me, so please scream this morning, okay? And scream real, real loud, because then I know you love me a lot!" When they arrived at the center, her daughter announced that she could walk in by herself. She probably didn't want to be seen with a mother who'd obviously gone over the edge. In any case, there was no more screaming.

A reader sent in what I thought was a great solution to getting a toddler to cooperate with being put in a car seat: She suggests parents purchase a second car seat in which to strap the child's favorite teddy bear. Strap "teddy" in first, she says, then the child. Makes great sense!

Q Just as sure as I tell my two-year-old not to do something, like write on the walls or put toys in the toilet, he turns around and does it. What can I do to make him stop testing limits?

A You're asking the wrong question. You don't really want your two-year-old to stop testing limits. You want him to stop repeatedly testing the same limits. Can you imagine what it would be like to live with a child who never tested limits? Peaceful, you say? Don't kid yourself. It would be boring and more than a little frightening. A child who never tested limits would probably sit around the house all day doing nothing. He wouldn't be uncooperative; but then again, he wouldn't be much of anything. So, twos test limits and may they do so forever. Why do they test them? Because they're there!

Jean Piaget found that a child's intellectual growth occurs in stages. During infancy and early toddlerhood, the child's understanding of the world is coded in his brain in the form of sensory and motor information. As language develops, the child seeks to match words with concrete experiences and things. For every word, the child "reasons," there must be a corresponding thing or event, and the child searches until the match is made. This means, among other things, that a child cannot understand a rule until he tests it, acts it out. So, "don't write on the wall" results in a mural on the staircase, and "don't put toys in the toilet" results in a visit from the plumber.

From another perspective, testing limits is an expression of creativity, initiative, and will. The child is responding assertively to a challenge, thereby strengthening his desire to achieve. I don't mean to romanticize testing and discount the very real problems associated with it. I simply want to emphasize that there's more here than meets the eye.

The question, however, remains: What's the best way to handle a toddler's limit testing so as to prevent ad infinitum repetitions of the same test? As I've said earlier, avoid use of the word "don't." Instead of saying, "Don't write on the walls," say, "Crayons are for writing on paper." If young Michaelangelo proceeds, in spite of your excellent communication, to decorate the walls, reprimand him and take the crayons away. The next time he wants crayons, ask, "What do you write on with crayons?" When he gives you the correct answer (as he probably will), give him the crayons (as well as some supervision).

Likewise, a child who insists upon straying out of the yard when he's been told not to should be taken inside. When he wants to go outside again, ask, "Where do you play?" Handled in this manner, limit testing will diminish naturally over time instead of evolving into a perpetual power struggle.

Q *Our thirty-month-old son is a typical "two." He's active, inquisitive, stubborn, and wants everything his way. At home, we manage to get by without major problems, but when we go into stores, chaos breaks loose. He climbs out of his stroller, runs away from us, plays in clothing racks, wants to touch everything he sees, and cries when we don't let him. Plus, every time we talk to a salesperson, he's underfoot, demanding our attention. Help!*

A This is exactly the sort of problem that requires "striking while the iron is cold." When you're in stores, you want your son to (1) stay in his stroller and (2) be quiet when you talk to salespeople. Two rules are as many as a two-year-old can keep in mind. Immediately before going into a store, you "strike while the iron is cold" by getting down on eye level with your little one and telling him what the rules are. Word them simply, because you also want him to repeat them to you. Then, into the store you go!

Now, when a problem occurs—say he gets out of his stroller—you can "strike while the iron is hot." If a misbehavior occurs, you again get down at eye level and say, "I told you to stay in your stroller. That's the rule." If he continues to disrupt, remove him to a quiet place in the store or leave the store entirely. Isolate yourself with him until he settles down, then go over the rules again, having him again repeat them. There are no instant solutions to problems with this age child, but if you are persistent and consistent, the lessons will slowly but surely sink in.

Q We have a four-year-old and an eighteen-month-old. They get along well—almost too well, in fact. The four-year-old is very active and boisterous— "all boy," so to speak. The problem is that the younger child is following in his older brother's footsteps. Together they run through the house, jump on furniture, knock things over, and screech at the top of their lungs. The older one seems to delight in the influence he has over his younger brother. They also seem to "feed" off one another. The more keyed up one gets, the more excited the other becomes, and so on. Do you have an anti-pandemonium solution?

A The eighteen-month-old is obviously getting his cues from his older brother, so if we can slow the four-year-old down, my hunch is the eighteen-month-old will follow suit. Let's give it a try.

Focus your efforts on the older child, and start with one rule, such as "no running in the house." Time-out is the technique of preference with a child this age. You'll need a portable timer and a relatively isolated place in which to put him for five minutes at a time. In and of itself, the place should not be punishing.

Once you have your "ducks in a row," sit down with your older child and say, "I want to talk with you about running in the house. I've told you I don't allow running, but you run anyway. When you run, your brother runs, too. I think it's wonderful that the two of you play so well together, but you're going to have to learn to play without running. From now on, when you run in the house, I'm going to put you in the downstairs bathroom and set this timer for five minutes. When the five minutes is up, a bell will ring (demonstrate how this works). You have to stay in the bathroom until you hear the bell. Do you have any questions?"

From this point on, whenever he runs in the house, all you do is say, "You were running, so you must sit in the bathroom until you hear the bell." When he comes out, say nothing about the incident, but if he should open the door or come out before the bell rings, put him back in and reset the timer. If you're consistent, he should stop running within a week or so. Once this is no longer a problem, add a second behavior, such as jumping on furniture, to the rules. Then a third, and so on.

If he asks why his younger brother doesn't have to go into time-out, tell him the truth: "I don't put your brother in time-out because he's not old enough. Besides, he's only doing what you do. If you stop running, he'll stop running, too." You should also tell him that it's his job, as an older brother, to be a "helper," and that the best way he can help you is to show his brother the right way to act around the house. With patience, you can turn his influence over his younger brother from negative to positive.

Q *We have two children: an eager-to-please eight-year-old and a hell-on-wheels thirty-five-month-old. The second child has always been difficult, but when he turned two, things went from bad to worse. He became so uncooperative we stopped trying to get him to do anything and fell into the admittedly bad habit of catering to him. It was that or be angry and in conflict with him all the time. Lately, he's started saying things like "I don't like my family" and "I don't like me." Are we seeing the beginnings of serious emotional problems? What should we do?*

A Your letter released a flood of memories. My son, Eric, was one of the most difficult toddlers I've ever seen. To keep the peace, my wife and I tried to avoid conflict with him as much as possible. We ended up swinging between catering to him and getting angry at him. Every time we got angry, we wound up feeling guilty. To purge our guilt, we'd cater, only eventually to get angry again. As you might imagine, our family was in a perpetual state of uproar. Through no fault of his own, Eric sat at the center of the cyclone.

One evening, shortly before Eric turned three, we went to the home of friends for a visit. We'd no sooner said our greetings than Eric suddenly announced he wanted to go home—now! We tried distracting, bribing, reasoning, ignoring. Nothing worked (it never did). Finally, he began to scream. We made our apologies, packed him in the car and drove home in silence, seething.

As we pulled into the driveway, Eric said, "You know what, Dad?"

"What?" I snapped.

"I don't like you."

It was devastating, like the Big Jury in the Sky had found me guilty for life. The more I thought about it, the more depressed I became. Eric, too, began to withdraw. In the midst of reading him a story, he'd suddenly ask, "What's wrong with me?" I felt an overwhelming sense of helpless heartbreak.

It was soon thereafter that Willie and I began taking control of our relationship with Eric. We stopped catering, bribing, reasoning, and threatening. We became, instead, unswerving in our expectations. As we did so, not only did Eric become more cooperative, but the cloud over him lifted.

Even the most uncooperative toddler wants to please. Parental approval translates to self-approval. Likewise, if a toddler senses a lot of parental anger and disapproval, he begins disapproving of himself. He expresses his confusion in statements such as "I don't like me" and, even more defensively, "I don't like you." This was, I'm sure, the crux of Eric's problem. I'd be willing to bet it's the crux of your son's problem, as well. The good news is that statements of this sort from a toddler are not so much signs of emotional problems as they are signs of a need for control, which this age child cannot provide for himself. The solution to your son's problem is called discipline, and the longer you delay confronting his unruliness, the worse things are bound to get.

Chapter 4

Adventures on (and around) the Great White Water Chair

*T*he mother of a thirty-eight-month-old recently told me, by way of explaining why her son had yet to learn to use the toilet, that his pediatrician had said children toilet train themselves "when they are ready." She interpreted this to mean that the mere mention of the toilet would not only be fruitless, but might also precipitate psychological problems. Unfortunately, professional advice along these same lines has become more the rule than the exception over the past decade or so. As a result, parents have been waiting, and waiting, and waiting, and in many cases, waiting long past the point when learning to use the toilet would have been a breeze for their children.

To be more accurate, this particular child's pediatrician should have told this mother that given proper support and encouragement, her son would, when he was ready, learn to use the toilet with relative ease. As concerns teaching a child to use the toilet, missing the boat will result in as many problems as jumping the gun.

Most of the problems that arise in the course of helping children pass this important developmental milestone can be traced to faulty attitudes and approaches. Many adults, for example, believe the central issue in teaching a child to use the toilet is cleanliness (hygiene). Not so. The crux of the matter is independence—the child's, that is. Learning to use the toilet is an exercise in "I can do it myself." For this exercise to work well for all concerned, the child must be given almost total control

over it. Parents need do little more than arrange things so the
child can use the toilet easily and be there to help when help is
requested. That's right, *requested*. It is generally wise to let the
child define when help is needed. Even the most well-meaning
assist, if not specifically asked for by the child, can set problems
snowballing.

Any child can be easily persuaded to use the toilet, and the
more low-key the persuasion, the easier the transition will be for
everyone. If, on the other hand, parents approach things with
the attitude that the child has a "bad habit" that must be "bro-
ken," the end results will be disastrous.

The term "toilet training" itself is part of the problem, because it defines parents as "trainers." A child will become toi-
let-independent more quickly if parents stay on the sidelines—
coaching, encouraging, and supporting, but *not* training.

As a parent, I tried it both ways, so I know what I'm talking
about. When Eric, our first, turned two, my wife and I decided,
quite arbitrarily, it was time for him to use the toilet. We put
him in training pants, bought him a child-size potty, and pro-
ceeded to hound him with "Don't you have to use the potty?"
and other equally neurotic questions.

The more we pushed, the less he cooperated, and the more
we pushed. As our frustration grew, we took to making him sit
on the toilet for long periods of time while we sat in front of him
reading stories, singing songs, and otherwise acting like fools.
Finally, after what seemed like an eternity, we'd let him up, help
him put on his pants, and send him on his way with admonish-
ments of "Don't you dare go in your pants!" It almost never
failed that within five minutes, he'd be standing in front of us,
soaked from the waist down, wearing a perplexed, "how'd this
happen?" expression. After four months of this, we finally "won."
I cringe to think of the havoc we created in the process.

Shortly after Amy, our second child, turned two, she began
showing signs of readiness. She began staying dry for hours at a
time and became curious as to what the rest of us were doing on
"The Great White Water Chair." Taking our cue, my wife and I
unpacked the potty, set it up in the den (where Amy spent most
of her time), pointed to it, and said, "When you feel like you
have to go poop or pee, sit on that, just like Mommy and Daddy
and Eric sit on the big potty. If you need help, call us." In two

days, she was self-taught, proving once again that the best teaching amounts to little more than simply pointing the way.

A Matter of Timing

The question parents most often ask about toilet training is, "When should we begin helping our child learn to properly use the toilet?" The answer depends upon the child, not the calendar. Some children are ready as early as eighteen months. Others show no signs of readiness until nearly age three. These, however, are exceptional examples. The majority of children are ready sometime between twenty-four and thirty months. Readiness demonstrates itself in three ways:

First, the child must be *physically ready*, meaning he/she has attained sufficient bladder capacity as well as command over the muscles controlling both urination and defecation. A child who's physically ready will be able to stay dry for periods of two or more hours during the day, wake up dry from naps, and possibly even wake up dry in the morning. In addition, the child's bowel movements must be fairly regular, and the child must show some sign of knowing when a bowel movement is impending.

Second, the child must be *intellectually ready*. This is reflected in an understanding of what toilets are for and obvious curiosity concerning them. The signs of intellectual readiness include wanting to watch people use the toilet (by all means, allow the child to do this!), wanting to flush the toilet, and asking questions about not just the toilet, but the process in general.

Third, the child must be *emotionally and motivationally ready*, meaning the child is able to communicate, however tentatively, a desire to use the toilet. The signs include sitting on the toilet (often fully clothed), wanting to sit on your lap when you use the toilet (let it happen!), and telling you when he or she needs to urinate or have a bowel movement.

The presence of all three readiness signs defines the most opportune time for learning toilet independence. This critical period usually emerges between twenty-four and thirty months. It varies approximately six months in either direction, and lasts from eight to twelve weeks, typically. During this phase, the child is "primed" for learning toilet skills and needs only support and encouragement from parents to do so. Again, "missing the boat"—failing to provide the proper support at the proper time—can result in as many problems as "jumping the gun"—pushing the child before readiness is there.

When the signs are all there, parents should make it convenient for the child to use the toilet and provide help when help is needed (requested, for the most part). At home, dress the child in training pants only, or even better, a nightgown or large, loose-fitting T-shirt with nothing on underneath. Put the potty near where the child plays during the day, even if that happens to be the kitchen.

Once the "props" are in place, say, "You have your own potty now. We want you to use it just like Mommy and Daddy use the big potty. Let us know if you need any help."

Parents should be role models and consultants to the child during this learning—available, but not hovering; helping, but not pushing. They should not, under any circumstances, follow the child around during the day, asking anxious questions like "Don't you think it's time you tried to use the potty?" When the child has an accident, as is inevitable, stay calm, reassuring, and supportive. Focus on success rather than failure, but keep praise low-key, lest you give the impression the child is performing for your benefit.

Questions?

Q *What if you're already guilty of "jumping the gun," and lots of problems have ensued? We tried pushing our son, shortly after his second birthday, into using the toilet. It's been six months now, and we've made no progress at all. In fact, any suggestion from us that he use the toilet results in no-holds-barred resistance. Furthermore, when he needs to urinate or have a bowel movement, he goes off by himself and secretively releases in his pants. Is there a way of going back to square one, or is it too late?*

A It's never too late with this age child to undo mistakes that have been made. In almost every case, more important than the mistake is the recognition that you made it, the willingness to correct it, and the determination not to repeat it. As a mentor of mine used to say, "The only mistake is one you don't learn from."

The first thing you need to do is back off. Prescribe a "cooling off period" for yourselves and your son. Be straightforward with him. Tell him you're going to stop trying to make him use the potty. Leave his potty, however, wherever it is in the house. In the morning, ask him whether he wants to wear diapers or "big-boy" pants and don't try to manipulate or guide the choice. If he indicates he'd rather wear training pants, help him put them on while restraining yourself from saying such "foot-in-the-mouth" things as "Wearing big-boy pants means you have to use to potty today, okay?" If circumstances demand that he wear diapers—if, for example, you're not going to be at home most of the day, and he's yet to show interest in the toilet—then don't give the choice. Just inform him that he's wearing diapers.

After initiating this "gag rule," the only thing to do is wait for signs that he's ready to take this important step toward autonomy. Remember, however, that when he's ready (and he will be, sooner or later, believe me), the learning will have to take place on his terms, not yours.

Q *I now realize that our three-year-old was showing all the readiness signs more than six months ago. We ignored them, thinking any action on our part would only serve to create problems. At present, although we're fairly convinced she knows how to use the toilet (and has, on occasion, for other people) she's all but oblivious to it when we're around. Is there anything we can do to turn back the clock?*

A Indeed, it's possible to "jump start" a child's interest in and willingness to use the toilet. If you think the skill is there, and are certain the interest was once there, all you need to do is provide the structure and stimulation to get the skill to emerge.

In situations of this sort, I often recommend using a "potty bell," consisting of nothing more than an inexpensive kitchen timer. Instead of encouraging her, at arbitrary times, to use the toilet, let the timer do your talking. I also have found it helpful, in situations such as this, to introduce the concept of "the doctor"—an outside authority figure that you invent for the purpose of conveying certain expectations.

Tell your daughter that you went to the doctor and he or she told you it's time for her to begin using the potty. Toward that end, tell her the doctor gave you a potty bell, which you then produce. Say, "The doctor says this potty bell will help you learn to use the potty. When you hear it ring, that means it's time for you to go sit on the potty."

Set the potty bell to ring five or ten minutes after she wakes up in the morning and from her naps. Otherwise, set it to ring (to heighten the mystery, don't let her see you) every ninety minutes to two hours, depending on what you guesstimate to be her "schedule."

When it rings, you say, "There's the potty bell! That means it's time for you to use the potty." At this point, it's important that you not prod. Simply point her in the direction of the potty, telling her to call you if she needs help. If she says she doesn't need or want to use the potty at that moment, don't try to persuade. Just say, "Okay, when you want to use it, you know where it is," and set the bell to ring in another hour or so.

Invoking the authority of "the doctor" is a creative way of preventing resistance to certain expectations you are trying to convey. I recommend using doctors over other authority figures (ministers, the police, television newscasters, the president) because doctors are regarded as so much larger than life in our culture that by the time a child is two-and-a-half, her perceptions of doctors have already been likewise enlarged. So, you want your two-year-old to go to bed at a certain time? "The doctor says this is when you should go to bed." You want your toddler to sit cooperatively in her car seat? "The doctor says that when you ride in the car, you have to sit in this seat."

And to anyone out there who thinks this runs the risk of creating a negative perception of or avoidance response toward doctors, think no more. We referred to "the doctor" quite often during Amy's early years, and she never demonstrated any fear of people in white coats. In fact, Amy always regarded trips to the doctor's office as an adventure (unless she knew she was getting a shot, that is). I'm not suggesting that the concept of "the doctor" be used threateningly, as in, "If you don't do what I want you to do, I'm taking you to the doctor and he'll have to give you a shot with the biggest needle he can find." Properly (and conservatively) invoked, "the doctor" becomes a benign means of bypassing power struggles.

Q   *Our twenty-seven-month-old daughter has just begun to use the toilet on her own. She is very proud of herself, as are we, but we want to be careful not to push. How much, if at all, should we remind her of the potty? Should we still put diapers on her at night, during long rides in the car, and when we're going shopping, or will this confuse her?*

A   As your daughter learns to use the toilet, she is also learning some important things about independence and responsibility—namely, that they both feel good. Therefore, the less involved you are, the better. Be a consultant, but not a participant. Remember that she is doing this for herself, and let her success belong to her. You don't even need to praise her a lot, because the reward comes from acquiring the skill. In fact, if you heap praise on her, she may stop using the toilet altogether. How else would she be able to get you to back off?

Reinforce the pride she takes in herself. Take her to the store and let her help you pick out some "big-girl" panties. When she's obviously looking for some praise from you, give her a hug and a kiss, but don't act like a cheerleader. Likewise, treat her inevitable accidents matter-of-factly and with words of understanding and encouragement. Let her tell you how involved she wants you to get. She will almost certainly need some help from you in learning to clean herself properly. Beyond that, you can tell her to call you if she needs you.

Continue using diapers at night for a while, but try a few nights without them every few weeks to see if she remains dry. Night dryness usually follows successful daytime toilet learning by three to six months. Don't give any reminders at all unless some major interruption of her routine is about to take place. These would include long car rides and trips to shopping centers. During car rides, stop every couple of hours and say, "It's time for all of us to use the potty." In shopping centers, show her that the stores have bathrooms and say, "Be sure to let us know if you need to use one."

Above all else, remember the musical maxim: She's gotta do it *her way.*

Q *Our almost-three-year-old daughter learned to use the toilet, and pretty much on her own, shortly after her second birthday. After nearly a year, however, she is still not consistently dry at night. She might go two or three nights without an accident, then wet every night for two weeks. As a result, we continue to put her diaper on at bedtime. Is there some way of helping her learn to stay dry at night?*

A I'd suggest you put your daughter to bed without diapers. During her first two years of life, the feel of wearing a diaper became associated with permission simply to release when her bladder became full. As she taught herself to use the toilet during the day, she consciously supressed that association. Ah, but it's still there, snoozing beneath the surface of her conscious mind. As soon as she falls asleep, it wakes up and "takes over." Wearing a diaper to bed, therefore, makes it all but inevitable that she'll wet in it.

Furthermore, the mere fact that you put a diaper on her at bedtime tells her you don't expect her to be dry through the night. Children tend to behave in accordance with the expectations their parents convey, however implicit (unspoken) those expectations may be. In a sense, by continuing to put diapers on her at night, you're giving her tacit permission to wet in them.

For the time being, and until she is consistently dry through the night, I'd recommend that you put her to bed in a loose-fitting nightie with nothing on underneath. This will increase the likelihood that she will be sensitive to the pressure of a full bladder while she's sleeping and "hold" until she wakes up.

Q *Our three-year-old daughter was successfully toilet trained at twenty-seven months. About a month ago, she began having bowel movements in her pants. At first, we thought she might have a physical problem, but her doctor says she's perfectly healthy.*

At his advice, we started making her sit on the toilet for thirty minutes after every meal and whenever she looked like she needed to go, but that didn't work. Now, when she has an accident, which is nearly every day, we clean her up, spank her, and put her in her room for a while. This isn't working either. What will?

A A regression in toileting skills such as you describe is usually triggered by a major change in the child's life: a move, parents separating, the birth of a sibling, or the start of day care. In some cases, however, the problem begins spontaneously, without apparent cause. Whatever the reason—or lack of one—it's important to realize that your daughter is not doing this manipulatively, to get attention or engage you in a power struggle. Young children don't think like that. They *respond* to attention, and they fall into certain behavior patterns as a result of attention, but they don't consciously think in terms of getting it. In all likelihood, she had an accident, you made a big deal over it, and she had another one. The more of a big deal you made of her accidents, the more of a big deal they became.

I can understand your frustration, but frustration does nothing but bring out the worst in parents. It muddles their thinking and causes them to do things that make problems worse instead of better. Punishing your daughter will do just that, as you've already discovered. Instead, give her responsibility for the problem.

First, review things with her: "When you were a baby, you wore diapers and pooped in them. Then you learned to use the potty and started wearing 'big-girl' panties. Now you've started pooping in your pants again, like when you were a baby. You've forgotten how to use the potty, so Mommy and Daddy are going to help you remember, which is what mommies and daddies are for. Yelling at you and spanking you isn't going to help you remember. Instead, when you poop in your panties, we're going to take you to the bathroom and leave you there to clean yourself up and rinse out your panties. Being in the bathroom and cleaning yourself will help you remember to use the potty next time."

Teach her how to swish her soiled panties around in the toilet until they're fairly clean and hang them up to dry.

Teach her how to clean herself, as well. (You may also want to keep a supply of clean underpants in the bathroom for her.) These are things three-year-olds can be taught to do. It isn't important that she do a perfect job, however. What's important is that she accept the biggest share of responsibility for the problem. From this point on, when an accident occurs, respond calmly: "Uh-oh, you forgot again. You need to go to the bathroom and wash out your panties and clean yourself like I taught you."

In anywhere from a few days to a few weeks, your patience and the fact that you've put the problem gently on her shoulders will begin to pay off.

Chapter 5

No More Bedtime Blues

*B*edtime. Two-year-olds, generally speaking, don't like it; parents are intimidated by it; professionals make careers out of speaking and writing about it. But despite its reputation as a psychologically complex affair, bedtime is nothing more than a disciplinary opportunity—a chance for growth in the parent-child relationship.

In this case, the growth involves the all-important step of parent and child learning to separate from one another. Like toilet training, where the issue is autonomy (a combination of independence and mastery), bedtime is precedent-setting. How the parent responds, emotionally and behaviorally, to this age child's almost inevitable resistance to being put to bed and left alone to fall asleep will have long-standing influence on how the child will process and react to other separation events (being left with sitters, going to day care for the first time, going to school, etc.).

If, for example, a mother interprets her eighteen-month-old son's protests at bedtime as evidence she's done something *wrong*, and responds by lying down with him every night until he's asleep, he's all but certain to protest every time his mother tries to separate from him, no matter the circumstances. The end result: a mother who feels increasingly guilty and insecure, and a child who is emotionally snagged at this developmental juncture.

On the other hand, if this same mother accepts her son's protests as the price everyone must pay to clear this hurdle, and continues to communicate firmly—but gently—that he must go to bed at a certain time and fall asleep on his own, the hurdle will eventually be cleared, to the lasting benefit of all concerned.

Like any other disciplinary opportunity, bedtime involves setting limits. To set limits effectively, a parent must communicate effectively. This requires that the parent have the child's undivided attention. Securing the attention of children requires that parents understand the stages of childhood. Disciplinary methods that work with a child at one stage will not always work with a child at another. More specifically, what works to solve bedtime problems with a child of thirty-four months is not likely to work with a twenty-two-month-old, and vice versa. Why? Because although only sixteen months apart, they are at vastly different points in their development. They each look at, understand, and relate to the world in their own unique ways. Solving bedtime problems with each of these children requires that their parents appreciate the uniqueness of each child's developmental status and fit their solutions to it.

Bedlam at Bedtime

Shortly before her third birthday (she's now twenty-one), our daughter Amy turned bedtime into a game of "Let's See Just How Crazy You Can Make Your Parents." Five minutes after we tucked her in bed, she'd be downstairs, asking "When's my birfday?" or "What're you talkin' 'bout?" or "Who was in the truck that jus' went by the house?" We'd answer her question, lead her back to bed, tuck her in, go downstairs, and wait. Sure enough, five minutes or so later she'd be standing in front of us, looking as innocent as a kitten.

"What is it, Amy?"

"Ummmm, I forgot to tell you somethin'."

"What did you forget to tell us, Amy?"

"Ummmm, I, ummmm, watched 'Mr. Rogers' today."

And back to bed she'd go (not of her own free will), until she thought of something else to ask or tell, or a reason to be scared and call for us, or a request, as in "I need orange juice!"

By ten o'clock, our patience having run out, one of us—usually me—would experience cerebral meltdown. I'd start babbling incoherently and, eyes glowing red, would chase Amy back upstairs, beating my chest like something out of *Where the Wild Things Are*. This would terrify Amy so much she'd be up another two hours, crying. It was usually midnight before the house was quiet.

After several months of this, realizing that persuasion, threat, and fear were not going to work, we thought of a way to outsmart her (no small feat, since children this age are much, much smarter than their parents). One night, while tucking Amy in, I leaned over and whispered, "When we leave your room, Amos, you can fool us by quietly closing your door, turning on the light, and playing with your toys. If you're berry, berry quiet, we won't hear you! Mommy and Daddy will think you're asleep, and we won't get mad, and you can play until you fall asleep!"

Her eyes got big and she giggled. "But if you make a noise, or open your door," I went on to say, "then we will have to put you back to bed and turn out your light. So let's see if you can fool us tonight, Amos. Let's see how quiet you can be."

Magic! From that night forward, Amy delighted in "fooling" us. Every evening, as we would tuck her in, we'd remind her of our gullibility. We'd share a conspiratorial giggle with "the Amos," as she is known, go downstairs, and revel in freedom from parenthood. A child's bedtime is, after all, for the sake of the child's parents.

Looking back, and knowing a lot more about children now than I did then, I realize that the invitation to "fool" us worked because it appealed not only to Amy's emergent imagination, but also to her desire to control her world—both of which, as you already know, are primary characteristics of this age child. Pleading, threats, spankings, and bribes had not worked because they failed to deal with Amy "at her level."

The "Family Bed"... Not!

Whenever I write on the subject of bedtime, I am likely to receive a flood of complaint from folks who believe in what is called "the family bed," from a book of the same title by Tine Thevenin, guru of the family sleeping movement. Thevenin, a Minnesota homemaker, "solved" bedtime problems with her two children by bundling with them. The family bed banner has since been taken up by the La Leche League and pediatrician Dr. William Sears, author of *Nighttime Parenting: How to Get Your Baby and Child to Sleep.*

The soap opera employed to justify the family bed is that children are traumatized psychologically by the act of being "abandoned" by their parents at bedtime. This trauma supposedly leads to all manner of emotional problems, the list of which is too long to cover in this chapter. Typically, the purveyors of this pseudopsychology go to absurdly melodramatic lengths to lay a guilt trip on parents who choose not to play musical beds every evening. Sample, for instance, the opening paragraphs to a 1981 *Parents Magazine* article extolling the virtues of family bundling:

> For thousands of American kids, every night is the loneliest night of the week come 9:00 P.M., when their happy, loving families turn abruptly into untouchables. Junior is sent to his lonely bed, freshly made up with Donald Duck sheets. After a brief kiss and a warning look . . . his parents avert their eyes, for there are few sights sadder than the thin back of a child as he goes off to face the night alone. His tiny wing bones quiver with betrayal, and there is that awful moment at the foot of the stairs when he turns to fix Mommy and Daddy with one last imploring look.

From that tear-jerking beginning, the author (a free-lance writer whose identity is irrelevant) drew on Thevenin and others to debunk some of the "myths" that lurk behind the oh-so-absolutely dreadful and destructive practice of putting children to sleep in their own beds, including the "myth" that sleeping alone promotes independence.

Trouble is, that's not a myth.

The point of assigning a specific bedtime for children and putting them ceremoniously in their own beds, in their own rooms, is twofold. First, it gives parents much-needed time for themselves and one another. Second, bedtime is an exercise in separation and, therefore, independence (also known as autonomy, self-reliance, and self-confidence). It is, in fact, the first of many such exercises to come. The manner in which parents handle it, therefore, sets an important and enduring precedent.

Separation always involves a certain amount of anxiety. It is often frightening for a child and, assuming his parents are sensitive and caring people, it will be discomforting for them as well. The problem of separation, of moving from dependency toward a state of confident self-sufficiency is, in fact, the primary problem of growing up.

In his best-selling book, *The Road Less Traveled*, psychiatrist Scott Peck says that many people never learn to accept the inherent pain of living. When confronted with a problem, they either attempt an impatient, knee-jerk solution or try to ignore it altogether. Parents who beat their children because they cry at bedtime fall into the first category. Parents who let their children sleep with them fall into the second. Both sets of parents have missed the point.

In Peck's terms, parents and children sleeping together is a way of avoiding a problem in the hopes that someday, somehow, it will miraculously resolve itself. Unfortunately, life will probably deal a different hand to "family bed-ers." The child whose parents avoid facing the pain of separation never receives complete, implicit permission to separate from them. As the years go by, his parents' continuing failure to confront and resolve this fundamental issue becomes an obstacle to healthy growth and development. In my professional experience and, I daresay, the experience of most other family psychologists, these children are generally dependent, demanding, excessively fearful, socially immature, and undisciplined.

At some point, nearly all young children cry at bedtime. Naturally, their cries make us want to draw them protectively closer. But protection of this nature is not always in a child's best interests. It is essential to the success of the emancipation process that children learn to deal with separation. Parents must show the way, and bedtime is one of the most opportune of places to begin the lessons. It's a big deal, to be sure, but as big deals go, not really that difficult at all.

In the following section, I respond to questions concerning bedtime typically asked by parents of toddlers. Because no one solution works for all children—even those of similar developmental status—I've made it a point to describe different solutions to problems that may appear similar, if not identical. It's up to the reader to choose the solution that seems to best fit the particulars of the situation as well as the personalities of the people—adults and child—involved.

Questions?

Q *I must disagree with your opinion on the subject of children sleeping in their parents' beds. What law or reason, other than "society," demands this unnatural practice? Isn't it true that, prior to this century, children had been allowed to sleep in or beside their parents' beds since prehistoric times?*

A Sleeping in his or her own bed helps establish that the child is an independent, autonomous individual, with a clearly separate identity. In addition, parents sleeping together and separate from the child enhances the child's view of the marriage as not only a separate entity within the family but also the most important relationship within the family. A child who sleeps with his or her parents is in danger of not achieving this understanding, of feeling wrongly that the marriage is a "threesome." It's important that a child understand that his parents' marriage is exclusive and, therefore, does not include him. This distinction positions the marriage at center stage in the family, at the focal point of attention. Coming to grips with the fact that the husband-wife relationship is paramount in the family helps the young child divest of self-centeredness, acquire a sense of independence, and move securely toward eventual emancipation. A child cannot achieve autonomy unless parents first establish the autonomy of their marriage. Autonomy is virtually synonomous with self-esteem. Therefore, what may look like a very nurturing arrangement—the "family bed"—actually extends dependency and interferes significantly with emotional growth. In short, I am absolutely convinced that my position rests on firm clinical and developmental ground, as opposed to simply being an extension of societal expectations and prejudices.

Regarding the historical antecedents of this issue, I think I'm correct in saying that in other cultures and other times, children have slept with their parents only when there were no other options. For instance, it would have been impractical, perhaps even deadly, for our prehistoric ancestors to hold out for nothing less than a three-bedroom cave. Nor does it make sense for nomadic peoples to lug three-bedroom tents from site to site or Eskimos to waste valuable time and energy building three-bedroom igloos. In our own culture, where you find, or found, children sleeping with parents, it is/was usually out of necessity rather than out of choice (as in the frontier family, living in a one-room house).

The fact that a certain child-rearing practice is or was common to more primitive cultures may qualify it as more "natural," but let us not confuse "natural" with most desirable or healthy. If the two were synonomous, our expected life spans would not have nearly tripled over the course of historical time.

The characteristics of the particular culture dictate how this issue will be handled. Perhaps cultures where children usually sleep with their parents have evolved other means of "cutting the cord." The adolescent puberty rites of some native cultures would be a prime example. One South Pacific culture initiates thirteen-year-old boys into manhood by having them dive off a hundred-foot tower with only a vine secured to their ankles breaking their falls. Does the fact that this rite is practiced by an aboriginal culture qualify it as more "natural"? If so, then perhaps we should not only all be sleeping with our children, but requiring all male children to bungee jump their way to manhood at age thirteen. My point is that a culture's child-rearing practices are designed to sustain that culture, and that culture alone. To say that one culture's child-rearing practices should be adopted by another is nothing short of naive. Western cultures tend to value autonomy and individual achievement. The separation of parents and children at bedtime is, I am convinced, conducive to this goal. It is, therefore, not only functional, but quite necessary to the Western child's proper social adjustment.

Given the choice, I'm certain that most young children would choose to sleep in their parents' beds as opposed to their own. But children will always choose ice cream over spinach, too.

Q *Do you feel the same way about letting a young child crawl into his or her parents' bed in the morning? Also, should the parents' bedroom be generally "off-limits" to children?*

A Ah, yes, all rules have their exceptions, and this one, too, can be suspended under certain special circumstances. These include when the child is ill, or is recovering from an experience that has temporarily upset his or her security (the death of a pet, for instance), or for a night or two after the family have moved to a new home, thus giving the child time to adjust to the new surroundings. No problem, either, with letting a child crawl into bed with parents in the morning for some "cuddle time." I see absolutely no parallel between this and letting children share the marital bed on a nightly basis. The one is playfully innocent, the other indulgent and insidious. When they were younger, both of our children occasionally got into bed with us in the morning. Amy continued doing so until she was a preteen, when, as is typical of children this age, she suddenly decided she wanted nothing at all to do with us.

On your question concerning the sanctity of the parents' bedroom, this is an individual decision. My personal feeling is that the parents' bedroom should, in general, be off-limits to children. Our children had to have permission to enter our room. But then, we extended the same rule of courtesy to them concerning their rooms. As they got older, the rule relaxed and eventually became: If our door is closed, you may not come in unless you ask permission, but if the door is open, *"mi casa es su casa."*

Q *Our eighteen-month-old daughter won't go peacefully to sleep at night. As soon as she hits the mattress, she begins to wail, and wail, and wail. We've even tried keeping her up until she's absolutely exhausted, but the wailing still results. Don't tell us to let her "cry it out," because we just can't. Besides, she's already proven she can scream nonstop for almost an hour. The only thing that seems to work is rocking her to sleep, which takes about twenty minutes, then staying in there and rubbing her back for another ten or fifteen minutes once we put her in the crib. The added problem is, if she goes down crying, she almost always wakes up screaming in the middle of the night. There must be a better way!*

A Indeed, there is a better way to put an infant to sleep. Known as "Rosemond's Guaranteed No-Mo Sleepless Nights," it consists of three easy steps to permanent nighttime bliss, while at the same time answering forever the question, "How do you keep 'em down in the bed after they've seen the alternative?" Here 'tis:

• Set a definite bedtime and stick to it. Do not, I repeat, do not, try to wear an infant down by keeping her up long after reasonable people have gone to bed. Contrary to popular belief, the later you keep an infant up, the more agitated she will become and the more difficult bedtime, when it finally arrives, will be. Instead of waiting for a signal from your daughter that she's ready for sleep, make the decision for her. Somewhere between seven-thirty and eight-thirty in the evening is probably reasonable.

• Thirty minutes prior to bed, start putting her through the preliminaries, which might include a bath, a snack, and a story. When the appointed hour arrives, put her down with a brief tucking-in ceremony and promptly leave the room, screams notwithstanding.

• Assuming she does, in fact, scream, go back to her room every five minutes and repeat the tucking-in ceremony. If you must, lay her back down, reassure her that the world as she knows it still exists, that you are still a part of her life, kiss her, and exit stage left. Do not pick her up and do not stay longer than one minute. Five minutes later, if she's still at it, go back in and repeat the procedure. Five minutes later, if she's still at it, repeat the procedure. Get my drift? (I'm going to stop here and mention that I've been accused of "pirating" this method from a relatively well-known book on children's sleeping problems. *Au contraire*. I can assure the reader that I described this method in my newspaper column at least two years before that book was published.)

• Sooner or later, your daughter will begin to tire of this foolishness and her screams will turn to whimpers. At this point, you should extend the interval to ten minutes, or whatever your common sense and intuition advise. If, however, she shifts back into full throttle, return to the five-minute plan. True, she may scream for a couple of hours at first, but after several nights of this, she will scream less and less with every passing night. After a few weeks, she will scream at bedtime for only a few minutes, if at all. Look at it this way: At present, you spend anywhere from forty-five minutes to an hour getting her to sleep, more if you count the fact that you are keeping her up much too late to begin with. With the method just described, if she screams for two hours, you will have gone back into her room no more than twenty-four times, for less than a minute each time. This means you will spend only twenty minutes or so putting her to sleep—an immediate 50 percent reduction in the time you spend putting her to sleep!

• Should she wake up in the middle of the night, repeat the "five-minute plan" until she falls back to sleep. Because she is, in fact, likely to wake up in the middle of the night for at least the first few nights, I'd recommend that you initiate the plan on a Friday night, or some other night when you don't have to go to work the next morning.

Lest you have any lingering doubts, I've been pushing this plan for at least thirteen years, and it's yet to fail (when parents hang in there, that is). Just call me "The Sandman."

Q When we put our eighteen-month-old daughter to bed, she gets on her hands and knees and rocks back and forth, gently banging her head into the headboard. If one of us stays with her and sings her a song while rubbing her back, she doesn't do it. If we leave her room before she's asleep, however, she'll cry for a minute or two and then start rocking and head banging. This has become distressing to us. We're worried that the repeated banging could cause damage. Furthermore, we don't understand why she would deliberately hurt herself. Is her head banging an expression of frustration?

A You're making this much too complicated. Lots of infants and toddlers put themselves to sleep by getting on their hands and knees and rocking back and forth. In the process, some accidentally discover the pleasures of head banging. I've even heard of children who have continued to do this—

albeit in slightly modified form—well into their elementary years.

In some mysterious way, the combination of the rocking motion and the gentle cranial stimulation helps these kids fall asleep. In this sense, it's what's known as a *transitional activity*, one that, in this case, assists the child in moving from being awake to being asleep. Children who invent activities such as these for themselves may have a generally easier time making transitions than children who are less resourceful.

Why rocking and head banging? Who knows? It's easy to understand how the rocking motion would be soothing, but the head banging is a bit more difficult to explain. Perhaps these kids have discovered a relatively harmless way of slowly knocking themselves unconscious. All kidding aside, it's nothing to fret over. You haven't done anything wrong, and contrary to your fears, your daughter isn't going to inflict brain damage on herself. It's not a nervous habit, nor is it a symptom of insecurity, frustration, low self-esteem, or worms. Much better for all concerned that she put herself to sleep in this manner than to become dependent upon being rocked to sleep by one of you at bedtime.

I'm fairly certain that bedtime head-bangers experience no pain whatsoever. Remember that a young child's skull is fairly elastic, more like cartilage than bone. It absorbs impact much more efficiently than our hard heads. What looks painful to us is probably quite pleasurable. I've never heard of bedtime head-bangers looking punch-drunk in the morning.

Q *Our twenty-two-month-old son has recently developed a sleeping problem. He's always been easy to put to bed and began sleeping through the night at an early age. Lately, however, he has been waking up two or three times a night. He gets out of bed, stands in the doorway, and whimpers until one of us gets up and puts him back in bed. He doesn't fight us. In fact, he falls back to sleep quickly and quietly. Getting up several times a night is becoming a real hassle, but if we ignore him, he just gets louder and louder until we give in. One night, I got mad at him, and he became upset and kept us up for nearly two hours. What could be causing this problem, and what should we do about it?*

A The "problem," if you insist upon calling it one, is the result of two influences. The first occurs sometime toward the end of the second year of life, when most children cycle through a phase of separation anxiety that usually lasts about three months. During this time, the growth of independence seems to stall and the child's requests for reassurance and closeness increase. Parents of children this age often describe them as being more clingy and whiny. This brief developmental glitch remains a mystery, but studies have shown children will get over it more quickly if their parents simply give them the reassurance they're asking for. The second influence has to do with neurological developments that are occurring around this time—developments which, among other things, cause changes in the child's sleep patterns. As a result, it's not at all unusual for a toddler who has been sleeping through the night suddenly to begin waking up one or more times a night. As neurological development stabilizes, the child's sleep pattern will follow suit.

So, regard your son's sleeping "problem" as something like a growing pain—just one of those things that happen in the course of normal growth and development. And, like all other such things, if you handle it properly, it will pass in due time, leaving not a trace of ever having terrorized your nights.

Your son is no more used to waking up in the middle of the night than you are, and is just as upset about it, it would seem. After all, the world is a quite different and frightening place when all the lights are out. So, he sticks close to the security of his room and cries out for some reassurance. You should count your lucky stars. He could be wanting to get in bed with you or you to get in bed with him. He could be fighting going back to bed, or screaming his lungs out for an hour or so. Or all of the above. As it is, he's asking for two minutes of your time, two or three times a night. That's a total of six minutes—a small and temporary price to pay.

If you will simply go to him quickly and calmly, and gently put him back to bed with a few reassuring words, he'll get over this in a few months, max. If, on the other hand, you continue dealing with his night waking as if it were a behavior problem (ignoring him, becoming angry with him, etc.), it will almost certainly develop into one. The choice is yours.

Q *Our son turned two several months ago. We probably should have given him a separate bedroom long ago, but it's been more convenient to have him in with us (the second bedroom is upstairs). He goes to bed easily in his crib around nine o'clock and usually sleeps the night. Occasionally, however, he will wake up and want to get in bed with us. To further complicate matters, he's almost climbing out of his crib. First, how and when should we move him from our room to the second bedroom? Second, how and when should we make the change from crib to regular bed?*

A Your son is certainly old enough to make both transitions, but I'd take them one at a time, starting with the move to a regular bed. There's no mystery to accomplishing this. While he's still in your quarters, dismantle his crib and put a single-bed mattress on the floor. Let him sleep there until he gets the feel of it and is no longer rolling out. This should take a month or so. When he's over this first hurdle, put the mattress in its frame and let him get used to that.

For safety's sake, given the fact that the second bedroom is upstairs, I'd wait to move him out of your room until he is no longer waking up in the middle of the night. Even then, I'd put a child-proof gate at the top of the stairs. Better safe than sorry. When you feel comfortable with the whole idea, prepare his room, involving him as much as possible. When things are ready, move his bed (and him) in there with much hoopla. There. The job is done.

Q *Our thirty-month-old daughter won't let us out of her bedroom at night. We begin getting her ready for bed around seven-thirty. After her bath, a snack, and a story, we'd like to turn out her light and leave. No such luck. The minute we move toward the light switch, she starts to scream. We don't feel comfortable with just letting her cry it out, so we stay in her room until she falls asleep. Meanwhile, she opens her eyes every few minutes to check on us. There have been many times when she seemed completely*

*asleep, but woke up as soon as we got up to leave. What can
we do?*

A There is a simple, creative way of freeing yourselves from
"bedtime bondage." First, make a "picture story" of the
things you do to get your daughter ready for bed. Either
draw pictures that represent each step of the routine or cut
them from magazines. Include a bathtub (for taking a bath),
some food (for eating a snack), a toilet, a book (bedtime story),
and a bed (for going to sleep). Once you have your pictures,
arrange them in order on a strip of poster board and hang
this "bedtime poster" somewhere in your daughter's room,
where she can see it from her bed (perhaps over her bed).
You'll also need a portable kitchen timer.

Tell her that the pictures tell the story of how all children,
everywhere, go to bed. You want to convey the idea that bedtime is universal, rather than something done only to her.
As you begin her bedtime routine, point to the first picture,
asking, "What's the first thing mommies and daddies do to
help children go to bed?" It will help to get excited about
her answer, as in: "That's right! You're so smart! And smart
children know how to go to bed!" That may sound ridiculous, but two-year-olds like that kind of stuff, so do it anyway.

At every step along the way, take her to the bedtime poster
and ask what comes next. When you finish the story, set the
timer for five minutes or so, telling her, "This is a bedtime
bell. When mommies and daddies finish reading children
bedtime stories, they set this bell. When the bell rings, that
tells mommies and daddies they have to leave and turn out
the lights so children can go to sleep." Again, you create the
impression that every child in the world has a bedtime bell.
(Note: Creating the impression that a certain practice or
rule—whether it relates to bedtime, mealtime, behavior in
public places, or whatever—is universal, is quite effective
with this age child. It makes things less personal and, as
such, reduces the likelihood of resistance.)

After setting the timer, sit next to her and talk quietly about
what happened that day. When the bell rings, tuck her in,
give her your kisses, and exit. The likelihood is she'll accept
bedtime as a matter of fact, but if she still screams, then

take turns "checking in" every ten minutes or so. Walk casually into her room, reassure her everything's all right, give her another kiss, and walk casually out, disregarding her protests. This whole operation should take no longer than thirty seconds. Eventually, she'll get the message and go off to sleep. After a couple of weeks, "bedtime bondage" will be a thing of the past.

Q Brian, our two-and-a-half-year-old, usually goes to bed at eight-thirty without a fuss and sleeps through the night. My husband's job takes him out of town one or two nights a week. Within the last few months, Brian has had a problem going to bed by himself when his daddy isn't home. Instead of going quietly to sleep, he cries and says he wants to sleep with me. I don't feel right about letting him in our bed because I don't want this to become a habit, but I've given in to him on occasion. My mother and several friends have advised that I let him cry it out. What do you think?

A I have a hard time with words like "never" and "always." More often than not, they're used to transform generally true statements into complete falsehoods. In this case, the generally true statement is "children belong in their own beds." The complete falsehood is "children should *never* be allowed to sleep with their parents."

In Brian's case, I see no reason why he shouldn't be allowed to sleep with you when Dad's out of town. Brian is seeking additional closeness with you as a way of calming the anxiety he experiences at his father's absence. This anxiety is a temporary thing, I assure you, as is his insistence on sleeping with you during those times. The more reassurance you give him, the easier it will eventually be for him to deal with these interruptions in the family routine.

Q Our almost three-year-old will go to bed without much trouble, but in the middle of the night he comes into our room and crawls in between us. If we tell him to go back to his room, he begins to cry, which is not a pleasant sound at three in the morning. More often than not, we're too tired to go through the hassle of taking him back to his room and putting him in his bed. After six months of letting him get in bed with us, how do we put a stop to it without making him cry?

A You can, with some effort, get him to sleep the night in his bed. Or you can, with no effort, prevent him from crying in the middle of the night. But you can't have it both ways. If you decide, as you should, that he must stay in his bed all night, he'll cry because you're taking control of a situation he has controlled for nearly six months. During that time, he has acquired the belief that his well-being at night depends on being in bed with you. By making him stay in his bed, you will temporarily disrupt his sense of well-being. Ultimately, however, making him stay in his own bed through the night will provide him great psychological benefit. A child who learns to separate at bedtime will have an easier time with other separation experiences as well. He'll be more trusting of his parents and therefore more confident as he moves toward emancipation.

Begin by telling your son, shortly before bedtime, that he will no longer be allowed to make his "night moves." The conversation might go something like this: "Tonight, Billy, you are going to stay in your bed all night long. If you wake up and come into Mommy and Daddy's bedroom, one of us will walk you back into your bedroom and tuck you in your own bed, where you must stay until morning. This is new, and sometimes children have to cry about new things. Mommy and Daddy will see you in the morning, and everything will be all right."

Then, do exactly as you've said you would. A word of warning: Don't do *anything* until you are convinced that you no longer want him in your bed at night.

Q *Our thirty-four-month-old goes to bed fairly easily, but wants us to leave his bedside light on until he falls asleep. We've tried making Delbert go to sleep with his lamp off, his door open, and the hall light on, but he acts afraid, repeatedly calls us back into his room, and takes much longer to fall asleep. Nine out of ten times, if he has trouble falling asleep, he'll wake up in the middle of the night and call for us. The obvious solution is to leave his light on, but we're concerned that by catering to his fear in this fashion, we might cause him to develop a habit of needing a light on in order to fall asleep.*

A   I vote for the obvious solution. To begin with, it's unlikely Delbert will develop a debilitating addiction to sleeping with bright lights on just because you let him go to bed with a lamp on when he was almost three. Fears, especially those associated with the dark, are fairly common to this age child. They are a side effect of the otherwise miraculous flowering of imagination. Understandably, the young child is not in complete control of the imaginative process and sometimes it gets away from him.

    One way this age child deals with fears is to form attachments to "transitional objects" like teddy bears, favorite blankets, and bedside lights. These provide imagined protection against things that go bump in the night. In other words, the child's imagination, which invented the fear, is also capable of inventing a solution to it. By indulging the child's attachment to the transitional object of choice, you're not catering to the fear, you're letting it run its course. Under these easygoing circumstances, the child will develop no fixations, believe me. How many adults do you know who still cuddle with teddy bears? (And so what if some still do?)

    On his own, Delbert has come up with a solution to his fear of the dark—a way of controlling it that is, after all, more desirable than screaming or demanding to sleep with you. By allowing him his bedside lamp, you will strengthen not his fear, but his ingenuity, self-reliance, independence, imagination, creativity, and intelligence, not to mention his courage. Furthermore, he will go to sleep quickly and quietly, a joy for which many parents would turn on every light in the house.

Q   *We have two sons, one who just turned three and one who's fifteen months. When the first was a baby, we rocked him to sleep. As he got older, I began lying down with him at bedtime. With the second, I simply put him in his crib, kissed him, and left the room. If he cried longer than ten minutes, I went back in, reassured him, and left. If he continued to cry, I repeated this process every ten minutes until he was asleep. By the time he was six months old, he was going off to sleep without a whimper. The three-year-old, however, still gives us problems at bedtime. Both boys sleep in the same room. I put the baby to bed around eight o'clock. When he's asleep, I go in and lie down with the three-year-old. Depending on when he took his nap, he will fall asleep anywhere between nine and eleven o'clock. If I try to leave his room before he's asleep, he gets out of bed and follows me, crying. What do you recommend?*

A The method you used with your second child works well with children who can't, or won't, get out of bed. So, we need to come up with something new. Let's see . . . yes, I think . . . by gosh, I have it!

First, establish a regular routine for both nap time and bedtime. Nap time should be the same time every day, shortly after lunch. Simply tell your three-year-old this is everyone's "quiet time," and that as long as he's quiet and stays in his room, he can stay awake and play. Set a timer for an hour and tell him he must remain in his room until the bell rings. If he "jumps the bell," direct him back to his quarters. If he falls asleep during the hour (which he eventually will), turn off the timer but don't let him sleep past mid-afternoon. If he doesn't fall asleep, let him out when the bell rings.

Next, establish a set bedtime along with a fixed bedtime routine that starts immediately after you put the baby down. As you leave the room after tucking in your three-year-old, place a necklace of beads (or something similar) over the doorknob. Give him permission to come out of his room for whatever reason. But tell him that when he leaves his room, he's to take the beads off the doorknob and give them to you when he finds you. In this way, he "pays" for the privilege of getting out of bed.

The first time he comes out of his room, take the beads, give him whatever he wants (within reason), and put him back to bed. This time, as you leave, *don't* put the beads on the doorknob. This means he no longer has permission to leave his room. If he breaks the rule, take away an important privilege (going outside, watching television) the next day. If he obeys the rule, reward him with something special (but not extravagant)—such as a trip to the park—the next day. You will, of course, need to explain all this to him before you start the procedure. In the final analysis, however, this is something he'll figure out in due time if, and only if, you are consistent.

Q   *Our two-year-old started climbing out of his crib several months ago. Since then, we haven't been able to get him to stay in his room at bedtime. We tuck Foxworth in around eight-thirty. Before leaving his room, we tell him, in no uncertain terms, to stay in his crib and go to sleep. Several minutes later, he appears in the den, grinning from ear to ear and wanting to play. We scold him and put him back in his crib. Several minutes later, it's the same story. This goes on for an hour or more every night. Finally, one of us goes into his room and stays with him until he's asleep. At our pediatrician's suggestion, we left a night-light on and closed Foxworth's door, but he became terribly frightened, and things were worse for several nights thereafter. Do you know of a way to correct this problem?*

A   No. Nonetheless, I have an idea, so bear with me. First of all, I sense you've been very patient with Foxworth thus far, which is good, because nothing makes a bedtime problem go downhill faster than yelling and screaming. Unfortunately, a calm approach, while it doesn't make things worse, rarely makes them better, either. In time, this phase will run its course, but it's anyone's best guess when that might be.

As I pointed out in chapter 3 ("Creative Discipline"), it's difficult, if not altogether impossible, to actually *correct* a behavior problem with a two-year-old. To correct a behavior problem, you must be able to apply a consequence of one sort or another. Generally speaking, the most effective consequence is one that involves withholding privileges. But twos haven't acquired many privileges to speak of, and they don't pay a lot of attention to consequences anyway, so that sort of approach isn't going to bring home the bacon. That leaves you with no choice but to try and *contain* the problem. In effect, your pediatrician's suggestion was along these lines, and given a couple of modifications, I think it just might work.

Take Foxworth's bedroom door off its hinges and cut it approximately in half, leaving the knob in the lower portion. Then rehang it such that each half swings independently. After tucking Foxworth in at night, leave a night-light on and close the bottom part of his door. Give him permission to play quietly in his room until he's ready to go to sleep. This arrangement might make him a bit angry at first, but it won't scare him. If, after you leave his room, he stands at the barricade and howls his displeasure, go back every five minutes or so to reassure him and repeat the rules: "You can play in your room until you're ready to go to sleep, Foxworth old boy, but you can't come out." Given a show of confidence on your part, he should adjust to these new circumstances within a few days. Oh, and by the way, you may as well go ahead and move him into a bed.

Q *We are three families being tyrannized by one small child's sleeping habits. Two-year-old William is a generally sunny little person, but he will not go to sleep peacefully. His parents work second-shift jobs, so William spends his weekday evenings with one set of grandparents one week and the other set of grandparents the next. His parents wake him from his nap in the mid-afternoon to take him to wherever he's spending the night, so he's already cranky when he gets there. When he's put to bed, he begins to scream bloody murder. One grandmother rocks him to sleep, while the other lets him stay up until he falls asleep on the floor with his blanket and bottle. On weeknights, his parents pick him up at midnight and take him home, which begins the bedtime battle all over again. They usually just give up and let him sleep with them. I feel certain that William's bedtime problems can't be solved until we all agree to one approach. The questions is, which one?*

A You're absolutely right! Little William's bedtime problems cannot be solved until everyone is on the same track. I'd suggest:
• On weekdays, William should be taken to where he's spending the night immediately after lunch and put down for his nap there.

• His bedtime should be the same regardless of where he sleeps. Likewise, a set bedtime routine should precede the "tucking-in ceremony," which should be brief. He should definitely not be rocked to sleep, stay up until he's exhausted, or allowed to sleep with anyone. Put him down, tuck him in, and leave the room.

• If he screams, use the "five-minute method" described previously in this chapter. At first, his screaming may go on for a couple of hours, but if everyone handles him the same way, it will gradually diminish.

• Keep him in one place until morning. Moving him at midnight will kill the plan.

• If he wakes up in the middle of the night, which is likely until he gets accustomed to everyone's new way of doing things, use the "five-minute method" again.

No one will have a good night's sleep until William has made the adjustment to his new routine. In other words, consistent with the adage, things will definitely get worse before they get better. But if everyone will hang tough, light should appear at the end of the tunnel in a relatively short period of time. Just keep in mind that it's either stress for a few weeks or stress for who-knows-how-many more years. Take your pick.

Q   *After we put our two-year-old daughter to bed, she picks up her blanket, spreads it out on the floor in front of her door, gets her pillow, and goes to sleep on her "pallet." She is very content and gives us no trouble whatsoever about going to sleep. Should we allow her to continue doing this?*

A   Why not? As long as she doesn't come out of her room after you put her to bed, then, as John Lennon put it, "Whatever gets you through the night, it's all right, all right." Two close friends of mine have a four-year-old daughter who has been sleeping on a quilt on the floor in her room ever since she was a year old. Periodically, her parents ask her if she'd like a bed, or at least a mattress. The answer is always "no." She is, I daresay, one of the most outgoing and intelligent four-year-olds I've yet to meet. I'll say it again: Where bedtime is concerned, the only thing of real relevance is that the child accept separation from parents at a reasonable hour. *How* the child accepts is a matter of personality, and—in this case, at least—the child's personality should be allowed free expression.

Chapter 6

Territoriality and Aggression, or (Bap!) "Mine!"

Nothing so provokes adult anxiety, panic, anger, guilt (need I go on?), or all of the above, as seemingly unprovoked aggression on the part of young children. I say *seemingly* because, whereas there may be, from the adult point of view, no discernible reason for the aggression, there is always, from the child's point of view, a reason of one sort or another.

Let's get one thing straight before we venture any further: Aggressive children don't have bad parents, nor is anything *wrong* with them. Most aggressive behavior—no matter how "uncivilized" (biting, for example)—is *normal*. Some children are simply more inclined toward aggressive behavior than others. We refer to this inclination with the words *heredity, predisposition,* and *temperament.* In any case, it boils down to "they were (probably) born that way."

Some toddlers, more passively disposed, when a toy they're playing with is snatched, will sit helplessly and cry. There's nothing *wrong* with these children for crying. They were born that way. Other toddlers, more aggressively disposed, when a toy is snatched, will snatch back and clobber. These aren't *bad* children. There's nothing *wrong* with them, either. They, too, were born that way. Remember, it takes all kinds.

Dealing with an aggressive toddler requires that parents and teachers be, first, patient. Keep in mind that you're dealing here with Mother Nature, and the more you try to hurry her along, the more she's going to trip you up. At the same time, you must respond *assertively,* but not—I repeat, NOT!—*aggressively* to displays of aggression on the part of the child. You can't fight fire with fire. So, when a two-year-old bites, please don't bite him back. If he hits, don't spank him. Whatever form the aggression takes, stop it, remove the child from the situation, communicate emphatically that such behavior is not permitted, and stay with the child until he or she cools off enough to return to the group.

Returning to one of the themes in chapter 3 ("Creative Discipline"), aggressive behavior is one of those things you cannot, in all likelihood, *correct* until the child is older. Until then, you are limited to doing all you possibly can to *contain* it. I'll delve more deeply and specifically into this in the question-and-answer section at the end of this chapter. Meanwhile, let's take first things first.

Sharing

I get a giggle out of adults who try to force two-year-olds to share. This endeavor is no less absurd than expecting a child of three to know "right" from "wrong," or a child of four to recite the Gettysburg Address. Toddlers are territorial little people. The space in front of them, and everything within it, is "mine!" Intrusions into that territory threaten the child's self-concept and, therefore, provoke distress. The more passive child cries, the more aggressive child strikes out.

Sharing is one of those civilized things, like chewing with one's mouth closed, that parents are in a hurry for children to acquire. Unfortunately, children are in no equal hurry. Sharing must be taught by parents and teachers who are patient and understand that just as in learning to read or ride a bicycle, learning to share is largely a matter of *readiness.*

Parents can begin planting the seeds of sharing during infancy and toddlerhood by defining things in terms of to whom they belong; as in, "this book is Mommy's," "this hammer is Daddy's," "this toy is yours," and so on. In this way, the child eventually comes to understand the concept of possession. As a three-year-old, he is more likely, if he sees another child playing with something he wants, to wait or ask for a turn rather than simply snatch it away.

The game of "Put-and-Take," which involves handing an item back and forth between yourself and your infant or young toddler, is an early method of teaching the concept of taking turns. As your child grows, you can continue to reinforce this concept by taking turns putting the pieces into a puzzle, or turning the pages of a book, or adding blocks to a tower. You can also create spontaneous teaching situations by offering to exchange things with your child, as in, "I'll share my juice with you. Will you share a cookie with me?"

The ability to share develops in stages: A child first learns to play peacefully alongside other children, then to take turns, then to share without adult prodding. The most one can reasonably expect of two-year-olds, while they are still self-centered and territorial, is what's known as "parallel play." During this first step in the socialization process, two or more children will occupy the same general space, but will play independently, each doing his or her own thing.

Occasionally, one toddler will raid another's territory, provoking a brief, but intense, clash of wills. Battles of this sort can be more easily managed by grouping twos according to similarities in temperament. For instance, several relatively passive, easygoing twos can play alongside one another for long periods of time without conflict. On the other hand, a group of active, assertive twos will clash, especially at first, but will arrive at detente within short order if allowed to work things out pretty much on their own. In this instance, the role of the supervising adult is to prevent mayhem, not determine the "pecking order."

Expect real trouble, however, when passive toddlers are mixed with active, aggressive ones. The more assertive toddlers, sensing the advantage, will take it. The result: snatching, hitting, and perhaps even biting, all to the tune of a chorus of wails from the more passive children. In such instances, the worst thing supervising adults can do is punish the assertive children and comfort the passive ones. Refereeing of this sort will only make the conflict more intense, the imbalance more pronounced. Managing mismatches among young children demands that an adult get involved, at least temporarily, as a facilitator, a mediator, a "Peacemaker of the Sandbox."

By age three, children are usually more socially conscious and significantly less self-centered. Reflecting these developments, their play becomes more associative and interactive. Whereas twos play alongside one another, occasionally raiding one another's space, threes start playing *with* one another, forming their first friendships in the process. For all these reasons, three is the ideal age at which to start a child in nursery school. Studies have shown that children who come to kindergarten with a couple of years of preschool behind them display better social skills than children who spend their preschool years at home.

Three-year-olds are able to participate in group activities and take turns with play materials, but spontaneous sharing is still rare. For some threes, especially young ones, even learning to take turns continues to be a real problem. Helping a three-year-old (or even an older two-year-old) over this hurdle requires no more than a kitchen timer and some firm, yet loving, direction. Take two children who are playing together but having difficulty with give-and-take over some particularly interesting toy. With kitchen timer in hand, the supervising adult says, "We're going to use this timer to help you learn to take turns with that toy. I'm setting it for (three minutes initally, gradually increasing the time to five minutes). Billy, you can play with the toy until the bell rings, then I'll set the timer again, and Robbie can play with it until the bell rings." This simple technique provides the structure these children need to take turns. In most cases, once the toy has alternated hands a few times, the timer will no longer be needed (until the next conflict arises, that is).

By age three-and-a-half or four, if the necessary foundation has been properly laid, a child should be able to share and play cooperatively in most settings. Even the most well-prepared child, however, will have occasional problems with letting go of certain possessions, necessitating some adult guidance. Although it may at times be appropriate to insist that a child share, the basic rule to follow when helping children through problems of this sort is to propose solutions that result in neither child feeling like the loser. Above all else, keep in mind that a child's right to ownership of his playthings must be affirmed before he or she is going to feel comfortable sharing with other children. In advance of a friend coming over, it may be helpful to let a child put up several favorite toys he doesn't want to share. Once he's made his selections, remind him that you expect him to share everything else with the friend. By providing the child

with an "insurance policy" of this sort, you increase the likelihood that the interaction will go smoothly.

Questions?

*Q Our eighteen-month-old son is in a play group with two children
of approximately the same age. The problem is, he doesn't protest if one of them takes a toy away from him. Instead, he simply
bursts into tears. How can we teach him to "hold his own" with
other children?*

A The territorial instinct is stronger in some children than in
others. Therefore, some children are more dominant and
aggressive in play groups while others are more passive. The
difference is one of temperament and appears to be innate.
It would appear that your son is on the passive side of the
social-style continuum, and there's probably not much you
can do about that for now. Later, when he's four or five, you
can begin giving him guidance in dealing with more assertive children. Always keep in mind, however, that the only
person who can do anything about this interpersonal ineq-
uity is your son, and he's never going to do anything about
it unless *he* sees it as a problem. The fact that it bothers you
not only is irrelevant, but in the long run, can make matters
worse. The more your son sees that you are upset when
other children take advantage of him, the more he will look
to you to "level the playing field."

I'd advise, therefore, that you keep a respectable distance
from his relationships with other children. You and other
supervising adults can use the kitchen-timer technique I
describe earlier in this chapter to get the children to take
turns, but you're going to have to accept that some toy snatching is going to take place. When he comes to you for comfort, dry his tears and send him back into the fray with words
of encouragement. If a certain toy seems to be the focus of
lots of conflict, remove it altogether. If a child in the play
group becomes physically aggressive toward another child
(hitting, biting), remove that child from the group until he's
calm. Because you're dealing here with a mix of both pas-

sive and aggressive children, you're going to have to accept that there will be days when the group atmosphere is going to be fairly stormy.

Q *Last week, I picked up our twenty-two-month-old son to give him a kiss, whereupon he hauled off and hit me in the face and laughed. I put him down, knelt in front of him and said, "Don't hit your mommy!" He just smiled and hit me again. What did I do wrong?*

A You used the word "don't," which is one of the more abstract words in the English language. It refers to the absence of a certain action. In other words, when the brain hears something like "Don't climb the fence," it must first register the directive—"climb the fence"—and then cancel the order. Much too complicated for a toddler. When this age child hears "Don't hit your mommy," he actually hears two things: "Don't" and "hit your mommy." "Don't" does not compute. "Hit your mommy" does. Whammo!

Tell a toddler what you want him to do instead of what you *don't* want him to do. Instead of "Don't climb the fence," say "Get down." Sometimes, however, the opposite of the "don't do" is hard to figure out or cumbersome to express. When that's the case, as it is with hitting, just say "No!" firmly and with a stern look. So, the next time your son rears back to hit you, stop him (if you can) and say "No!" If you don't intercept the blow in time, take the offending hand firmly in yours and say "No!" Either way, he'll get the message. Eventually.

Q *Our two-year-old has started hitting us whenever he doesn't like something we've done to him or doesn't get his way. Is it okay to spank him or pop his hand when he hits us? If not, then what should we do? By the way, don't tell us to sit him in time-out, because he won't stay. As soon as one of us sits him down, he pops back up again.*

A First of all, you're describing behavior that's normal for this age child. Not that all two-year-olds hit, mind you, but enough do that it's normal. Hitting results when the flint of an aggressive two-year-old's personality strikes the iron of something frustrating.

No big deal, actually. Remember that twos are uncivilized. They have yet to learn the ins and outs of appropriate social behavior. When frustrated, they go with their first impulse. If the first impulse is to hurl themselves on the ground and scream bloody murder, then hurl and scream it is. If the first impulse is to hit, then hit it is.

I would not recommend that you spank or pop your son's hand when he hits you. While I'm not altogether opposed to an occasional swat to the bottom, my experience tells me that spankings usually create more problems than they solve at this age. A spanking is likely further to enrage an already frustrated child, setting the proverbial snowball rolling.

Instead, I recommend you use time-out. Wait! I know you said time-out doesn't work, but hear me out. You apparently think time-out only works if the child sits cooperatively until he's told to get up. In that sense, time-out definitely does not work with most twos, who, like your son, won't sit in one place longer than it takes for their parents to straighten up and take a step or two away. If, however, you don't make an issue out of how long the child sits, time-out can work quite well with even the most stubborn two-year-old.

The next time your son hits one of you, get down at his level, and with a stern look and a firm tone in your voice, say, "No!" Then, lead him to the nearest chair and sit him down, saying, "Sit here until I tell you to get up!" Take a quick step back and say, "You can get up." Then turn around and walk away. The trick is to tell him to get up before he gets up on his own. In this rather clever way, you prove your point, which is that you can move him, but he can't move you. By responding assertively (but not aggressively) to his hitting, you demonstrate your control over yourself, the situation, and him as well.

If you do that every time he hits you, he should stop altogether in a year or so. I'm just kidding. But seriously, don't expect a miracle. Twos are as persistent as all get-out (whatever that means), so hang in there.

Q *Our almost-three-year-old has recently taken to hitting us—or trying to at least—whenever he's mad at us for not giving him his way. We've tried explaining to him why he shouldn't hit and have suggested other ways of expressing his frustration, but he doesn't listen. His preschool teachers tell us he's well behaved and gets along well with other children. Furthermore, he's never even tried to hit anyone at school. We wonder, therefore, why he's so angry with us. We recently read an article in which a child psychologist recommended against any form of punishment for hitting. Punishment, she said, will cause a child to repress anger and learn that feelings are bad. She recommended that the child be given an inflatable "Bozo the Clown" that he can beat up on whenever he has angry feelings. Thinking this might help, we bought our son a "Bozo," but his hitting has since gone from bad to worse. What should we do now?*

A I never cease to be amazed at the rhetoric certain professionals invent to justify the positions they take on child-rearing issues. Encouraging children to vent their rages on inflatable "Bozos" is permissiveness at its worst and most absurd. When and how, may I ask, will a child ever learn to tolerate frustration and control his temper if he's never required to do so?

Growing up involves learning self-discipline, not only as it applies to behavior, but to emotions as well. Feelings are private, intimate matters, not intended for unrestrained public display. Teaching a child to control the expression of feeling is a far cry from repressing those feelings or teaching him that feelings are bad.

If, as his teachers say, he's generally well behaved and has never tried to hit anyone at preschool, then there's probably no deep psychological reason for his hitting. He hits you because he's angry at you for not giving him his way. Plain and simple. His frustration overwhelms him, his impulses take over, and he lashes out. He doesn't lash out at playmates or teachers because he can't predict their behavior as well as he can predict yours. It's "safe" for him to lose his temper with you, so he lets it all hang out.

When he loses control, it's your responsibility to control him. That's what parents are for. What does he need to know?

That you won't allow him to hit you. How can you get this across? Easy. Don't let him. Surely you can read his behavior well enough to know when he's about to hit. When the attack comes, demonstrate your authority and control by intercepting the blow. Take his hands firmly in your own and tell him that you will not, under any circumstances, allow him to hit you, as in: "You may not hit me, I am *not* giving you a cookie before supper (or whatever), and you are going to sit in this chair until I tell you to get up." At this age, a child will sit for a couple of minutes, but is more likely to cooperate in time-out if you use a kitchen timer to signal when he can get up. So, get yourself a kitchen timer, and when you put him in time out, set the timer, saying, "You will sit here until the bell rings."

Later, when the iron's no longer hot, you can talk authoritatively to him about his anger. Don't ask him why he's angry, please! Instead, make statements about anger and hitting: "It's okay to get mad when I won't let you do what you want, but it's not okay to hit. You can tell me you're mad and we'll talk about it. If you don't feel like talking, you can go to your room until you calm down. But I won't let you hit me, and when you try, I'm going to sit you in the chair. Do you understand?"

Meanwhile, make a present of the "Bozo" to a child who'll give him a good home.

Q *My two-year-old occasionally bites himself when he's angry. Does this mean he's insecure, or that something is troubling him emotionally? If not, what can I do to stop him?*

A While it's possible to "cure" a toddler of biting other people, it's virtually impossible to prevent him from biting himself. In the first place, you can rarely predict when it's going to happen, and even if you could, you wouldn't be able to move fast enough to stop it. Self-biting is somewhat like lightning, except this bolt from the blue will often strike more than once in the same place.

Parents become alarmed and confused by self-biting and generally respond with one form or another of uncivilized panic. They shriek, run for help, struggle to separate "Jaws" from arm, or faint. They're also likely to feel that in some theoretical way they have "caused" the child to bite himself, in which case the child ends up being held and pampered. As a consequence of all this drama and attention, the child begins to bite himself more and more often, and once again, a mountain has been manufactured out of a molehill.

When your normally uncivilized toddler bites himself, do absolutely nothing. Pretend to be busy with something else. If he shows you the bite mark, tell him how sorry you are that he hurt himself (but be matter-of-fact about it) and go back to your business. If he breaks the skin, calmly help him wash and apply antiseptic to the area. If there's any doubt in your mind as to whether he's adequately protected against possible infection, call his pediatrician. In any case, be nonchalant.

There are two answers to your question concerning possible insecurity: No, biting himself doesn't mean he's insecure, and yes, something is troubling him emotionally; namely, he didn't get his way. Some toddlers "teethe" on themselves, some don't. Those in the first category do so out of frustration. When they get a big reaction, they figure that biting themselves is a big deal and do it all the more. In an older child, self-biting may be indicative of a psychological disturbance, but in a toddler, it's just one of those things.

Q *We have two daughters, ages thirty-four months and twenty months. At first, the older child seemed to accept her younger sister, and things went well between them. Within the past few months, however, an often-intense rivalry has developed. While it's often hard to tell who started something, the older child clearly uses her physical superiority to her advantage. When they get into a scrap, it usually involves a toy. The older child knocks the baby down, snatches things away from her, and has even hit her on a couple of occasions. We don't want to be constantly reprimanding the older one, but feel we must do something when these altercations occur. Can you give us some guidelines?*

A It's important that you intervene as little as possible in their altercations. It goes without saying that you have to get involved when the baby is in danger of getting hurt. You might also need to intervene if conflict occurs in inappropriate situations (e.g., when you have guests) or becomes extremely disruptive. But if it doesn't sound like anyone is getting mangled, stay out of it. When you do get involved, do so in a way that doesn't assign blame to either of the girls. Don't concern yourself with who started it or who did what to whom. Take the toy away, or separate them for a time, or reprimand them both for making such a disturbance, or all of the above, but don't sympathize with one and punish the other. Although it's probably true that your older child is the aggressor, if you fall into the habit of assigning the roles of "villain" and "victim" to the children at this point in time, you will set the stage for never-ending and ever-escalating sibling rivalry.

If you handle their conflicts without assigning blame, then your second daughter will eventually figure out how to solve the problems posed by having an older sibling. Furthermore, time is going to all-but-eliminate the older child's physical advantage; so she, too, is going to have to find other ways of asserting herself with her younger sister. Have patience.

Q *How can we keep our thirty-six-month-old daughter from hurting our ten-month-old son? Ever since her brother started crawling, our daughter has been extremely rough with him. She picks him up and squeezes too hard, drags him around, pinches him, and yanks things out of his hands. The usual scenario begins with her picking him up to "love" him. Then she begins to squeeze and he begins to cry. When we reprimand her, she always says she's sorry and acts contrite. We are baffled. Is she doing these things on purpose or what?*

A The situation you describe is not at all unusual, especially when the space between two children is less than three years. At the time your son arrived on the scene, your daughter was not quite ready to give up the status of "baby" and the dependency that goes with it. Not only that, but being the firstborn meant she didn't have to compete with anyone for your attention for nearly two-and-a-half years. One can get used to that kind of privilege in a hurry, you know.

When her brother was born, your daughter probably thought he was interesting and cute. In his helplessness, he posed no threat. Then he began getting about on his own, and she realized he wasn't so helpless after all. At this point, feeling threatened, she began acting to consolidate and protect her territory and status within the family. In the process, she began hurting him.

That's not the whole story, however. Your daughter is in obvious conflict. On the one hand, she has genuinely loving feelings for her brother and wants to be close to him. On the other, when she gets close, her anxiety and frustration get in the way of her affection, and she winds up squeezing instead of hugging. Please understand that your daughter doesn't really intend to hurt. Her conflicting feelings just get in the way of her ability to be gentle.

Your first priority, of course, is to protect the baby. The trick is to do this without identifying your daughter as "bad." You also have to find ways of teaching her to be gentle and loving toward her brother. The approach I always recommend is to place the baby completely off-limits to the older child for a period of one to two weeks. During this time, it's important that you not allow your daughter to come within more than a few feet of her younger brother.

You might ask how she's going to learn to be gentle if she isn't allowed to go near him? The answer is based on the fact that when a certain privilege is withheld from someone, that privilege begins to look increasingly attractive. By keeping your daughter at a distance from her brother, contact with him becomes more desirable. But to have contact, she must learn the art of gentleness, which you're going to teach her. During this training period, have your daughter help you as much as possible with the baby by getting you things and doing things for you while you're occupied with him. When you feel it's time, begin allowing her brief moments of contact, which you carefully supervise. Let her give him a spoonful of cereal or hold him on her lap while sitting next to you, and so on. Guide her through several such exercises the first day, and increase the number of contacts she has with her brother on succeeding days. Praise her for being helpful and gentle.

Don't be alarmed if things go well for several days and then another "incident" occurs. This is likely to be a two-steps-forward, one-step-back process for at least several weeks. Eventually, however, your patience and your strategy will prevail.

Chapter 7

Day Care vs. Parent Care, or "Who's Minding the Store?"

*I*n the course of writing this chapter, I changed horses in midstream. My original persuasion was that a toddler, even an infant, can thrive perfectly well in the daytime care of a person or persons other than a parent as long as the day care is truly caring. I was prepared to argue that the single most relevant issue is the *quality* of the day-care experience. If the people who provide the care are committed (as opposed to simply punching a clock) and competently trained, and if the day-care environment is responsive to the child's need for affection, attention, exploration, and stimulation, then there is no reason (I was going to say) to believe the tot is any worse off than he or she would be in the full-time care of a responsible parent. For the past twenty years, that has been my position concerning this issue. But I've changed my mind. For reasons having to with the research I did during the writing of this chapter, I am now convinced that parent-care during the first three years of life is clearly in the best interest of a child. This is not the "politically correct" position, however, and for two reasons:

First, parent care is usually equated with mother care. Therefore, although it matters not, in my estimation, whether the parent providing the care is male or female, or whether two parents manage their schedules such that they split child-care responsibilities, many people will feel that my remarks are directed primarily, if not exclusively, at women.

Second—and being, for the moment, gender specific—a working mother is generally viewed as more "liberated" than a mother who opts to provide home care for her children. As a result, a significant number of people will view my remarks as downright regressive, tantamount to suggesting that "a woman's place is in the home." I will, no doubt, be accused of being criminally unenlightened.

The fact is, I am as much for women achieving self-fulfillment as I am for men. I believe that the best parents are, in fact, self-fulfilled. True self-fulfillment, however, is a mature quality. It is not reckless, impulsive, or driven by self-centeredness. A truly self-fulfilled individual does not disregard the needs of others or do things at anyone else's expense. Self-fulfillment, in other words, is not equivalent to self-gratification. In fact, a defining feature of maturity is the ability to postpone self-gratification. If, therefore, in order to provide at-home care for a young child, a parent or parents must postpone self-gratification, then so be it. More than anything else, children need parents who are able to make mature, responsible decisions.

The "Changing" American Family

For the past thirty years, the American family has been "changing," or so the media informs us. The subliminal impression thus created is that some natural, inexorable evolutionary process is behind the steady increase in single-parent and two-income families; further, that the only problem arising from this is the failure of society and government to make sufficiently rapid and effective adjustments to the new set of circumstances.

Here's the truth: For more than a generation, the American family has been in a steady state of decline, precipitated by social experiments and forces that are fundamentally at odds with a general state of family health. The past thirty years have made it clear that the American family cannot coexist with the expansionary policies of these social experiments. One must go (or at least be curtailed), or slowly but surely, the other will.

Here's another undeniable truth: The American family worked better when there was a parent in the home during the day. In past generations, that parent was almost always female, but gender is irrelevant to the purpose of our discussion. That all-but-constant adult presence provided for greater family stability, smoother internal transitions, more effective overall time management, better supervision and care of children, and more efficient delegation of responsibilities, not to mention a lower level of stress. The comfortable division of labor between homemaker and breadwinner was more conducive to a sense of partnership and, therefore, tended to support marriage-centeredness. For all these reasons, the American family of previous generations was a more psychologically secure place in which to live. This despite the assertion of a significant number of "helping professionals" that most of us were raised in "dysfunctional" families lorded over by parents who were abusive in one way or another.

The neofeminist movement, one of the social experiments in question, has succeeded at convincing significant numbers of women (and men) that there is no incompatibility whatsoever between career pursuit and child rearing. Reading a recent interview with a married professional woman who has two children, ages three and seven months, I came across the following statement: "I took eight weeks maternity leave with my first child, six with my second. I could have taken longer, but in my profession, that's not looked upon favorably."

Excuse me? You have children and you put them in day care as quickly as you can (six weeks!) because you might be put on the "mommy track" if you don't? What are children, anyway? Hobbies? This woman was actually presented as a role model—living proof that it matters not whether children are taken care of during the day by parents or total strangers. What matters is that women do it all!

The "Superwoman" of that interview represents a society that's had the wool pulled over its eyes. She embodies the myth that there are no consequences to a child of having parents who try to have their cake and eat it, too. In part because personal sacrifice has come to be viewed as just shy of degrading, we have become a nation of families in various states of fragmentation; families in which priorities have been inverted, everyone's in a perpetual state of hurry, and psychological resources are stretched to the limit. And families that don't fit this description are regarded almost suspiciously.

The American family is *changing*? That's a nice way of putting it.

Attachment

From day one, parent or parents and child are engaged in an almost constant exchange of sound and movement. This "dance" forms an emotional attachment that secures the child's trust in the environment. Trusting that the world is a safe, nurturing place, the child can begin the long journey toward emancipation with confidence, moving away from his or her parents and into the world. As he explores and experiments upon the environment, the child exercises and thereby strengthens competency skills. I would argue that in all but the most extreme cases there is no one more in tune with the child, and therefore more capable of properly responding to this process, than the child's parents. The good intentions of the most well-trained day-care workers simply do not compare. To this I would add that the only people who can properly help the child make the critical transition from self-centeredness to parent-centeredness during the second eighteen months of life are, as well, the child's parents.

For the last twenty years or more, the professional community has been engaged in a cover-up concerning these issues. Not wishing to offend anyone, much less appear out of step with the times, developmental psychologists, early-childhood educators, and the like have acted as if home care and day care workers were fundamentally equivalent. The impression created has been that if parents know what to look for in a day-care center, a young child will be as well off in the care of strangers for forty-plus hours a week, fifty weeks a year, as in the care of a parent. That's a myth. It's a myth that serves the needs of day-care providers, employers, and to some extent, women, but it's a myth, nonetheless.

Here's the truth, the whole truth, and nothing but the truth: Being cared for during one's tender years in one's own home by a responsible, committed parent is distinctly different, both qualitatively and quantitatively, from being cared for in even the best of day-care centers. If these are two distinctly different situations, then the outcomes to a formative-years child must also be distinctly different. We are naive to think otherwise. Having proposed what I believe is not debatable, I am simply convinced that a child's needs are better served in the former situation.

What, therefore, are the *possible* consequences of placing an infant or toddler in day care? First, lacking in care-givers who are adequately tuned to the child, the child may not develop a sufficient sense of trust. The environment, therefore, appears threatening, rather than nurturing and inviting. Insecurity prevents the child from moving creatively out into the world. Either the child withdraws, becoming depressed and clinging, or his explorations appear driven and chaotic, rather than creative and purposeful. In this regard, it is interesting to note that as the number of infants and toddlers in day care has increased, so has the incidence of childhood depression and behavioral disorders, including attention-deficit hyperactivity disorder (ADHD), which is characterized by a preponderance of driven, chaotic activity.

Whether clinging or driven, the child's ability to develop a fully strengthened complement of competency skills has been compromised. This sets the stage for the eventual development of a host of potential problems—behavioral, emotional, social, and academic.

Is it possible for a young child who is cared for during a significant portion of the day by a person or persons other than a parent to develop a positive perception of the environment and, therefore, a positive self-image? Possible, yes, but parents are throwing the dice whenever they entrust the day care of an infant or toddler to someone other than themselves. The first three years of life constitute the single most critical, precedent-setting of all developmental periods. Of utmost importance to the child's developmental integrity are parents who are first, available, and second, properly responsive to the child's needs during this time. During the first eighteen months of life, it is essential that the child be the center of his or her care-givers' attention. Without this confirmation of self-importance, the child will experience insecurity which, in turn, will handicap the emergence of creative behavior. Not only is it logistically impossible for day-care workers to place any one infant at the center of their attention, but consider also that day-care workers, despite generally sterling intentions, are not *emotionally* invested in the development of the children in their care. (This does not, however, mean they don't *care*.)

During the second eighteen months of life, it is equally essential that the child be slowly but surely guided toward the understanding that he or she is not the center of the universe. The only people who can properly guide the child through this upheaval are people in whom the child has invested tremendous trust. But sufficient trust only develops if the child has been the center of attention during infancy and early toddlerhood. Again, regardless of the level of their commitment, day-care workers just don't fill the bill.

Would some children be better off in the care of someone other than a parent? Definitely, but if you are reading this book, then you are not one of those parents. You are concerned, committed to doing the best job you can at raising your child, responsible, and caring. And yes, you are also flawed. Even the most responsible, caring parent will make mistakes, become frustrated, and lose patience. But despite your faults and your mistakes, you will do a far better job than someone who does not share your emotional commitment to your child, and your child alone.

Baby-sitters, Family Home Care, and Other Such Things

Am I saying that infants and toddlers should never be left in the care of third parties? Absolutely not! I am referring here to full-time day care, period. I do not mean to include baby-sitters, "Mother's Morning Out" programs, or even three-mornings-a-week nursery schools (or whatever they call themselves) in this critique. In fact, I am all in favor of parents making time for themselves and especially their marriages. And I am all in favor of infants and toddlers having experience with adult caregivers other than their parents. But I cannot, in good conscience, endorse putting a child of tender years in full-time—as in six to nine hours a day, five days a week—day care.

And so, you might ask, where does this leave the single parent who has no choice other than to hold down a full-time job? Why, it leaves her having to put her child or children in full-time third-party care. (Gender-specific pronouns are used because, although the number of single fathers with custody is increasing, the number of single mothers with custody is still significantly higher.) In that event, she should find the very best circumstances her day-care dollar can provide. The next best alternative to parent care is a family home setting in which the care-giver is looking after no more than two or three children. A small-scale home setting increases the likelihood that each child will receive sufficient individual attention, and because there is no rotation or staff turnover in a home setting, the infant or toddler can form a more secure relationship with the care-giver. Fewer children also means the care-giver can be more accommodating with respect to variances in sleep, feeding, and activity schedules. A home setting is also going to feel more familiar, and therefore less intimidating, to the young child. All this makes for a smoother and less stressful transition.

With a home setting, the parent usually enjoys greater access to, and better communication with, the actual care-giver. Also, the care-giver in a home setting can be more responsive to the parent's preferences concerning such things as the child's diet, nap schedule, and so on, than is generally possible in a larger group setting.

Since most states now inspect and certify day-care homes, the first question to ask a prospective home-care-giver is "Are you licensed?" While a license doesn't necessarily mean better care, it at least guarantees that the home meets minimum standards.

Group-care Guidelines

If the parent of an infant or toddler has no choice other than group care, then group care it is! In that event, the following considerations are important:

Child/staff ratio: The fewer children there are per full-time staff person, the more likely it is that each child will receive a more sufficient share of individual attention. For children between the ages of eighteen and thirty-six months (the focal range of this book), I recommend that the child/staff ratio be no more than four children per full-time staff person. Many day-care centers, and especially those that are part of national chains, cannot afford to operate with a ratio this low—another rationale for family home care.

Rotation and turnover: Consistency of care gives the young child more opportunity to form a relatively secure care-giver attachment. Do staff persons rotate in and out of the toddler room during the day? How long has the present toddler-care staff been at the center? The answers to these questions give some indication as to the quality of the work environment, the level of employee satisfaction (keep in mind that if employees are unhappy, they aren't going to provide a positive emotional environment for children), the level of staff commitment, and the overall stability of the environment.

Experience and training: How and where have staff persons been trained? What certificates do they presently hold? Is their education ongoing? How much experience does each staff person have working exclusively with toddlers? What is entry-level pay for a full-time teacher? The answers to these questions will tell you whether day care is a career or just another job.

Environment: The room should be bright and airy, with a neutral odor. There should be plenty of open floor space, as opposed to clutter, and there should be absolutely no "playpens." The term itself is a misnomer, as these confined spaces are nothing more than "holding tanks" that restrict exploration and, therefore, the emergence of essential developmental skills. They should be called "boring-pens." The play area should be stocked with simple play materials such as large blocks, dolls, and books. Overall, the room should invite exploration and discovery. There should be dress-up clothes that invite children to play pretend games and stretch their imaginations. In addition, there should be areas for water-play, rest, looking at books, and coloring and working with clay. There should also be an outdoor play area where children can run, jump, climb, swing, and ride push-tricycles—all in the name of developing good motor coordination and a healthy appetite.

Attitude and disciplinary style of staff: Teachers are active, involved, and responsive, as opposed to just standing around. They look relaxed, yet "on their toes." In general, they look like they enjoy their job and love working with children. When discipline is needed, the staff responds firmly, yet lovingly. They are attentive enough to ward off the majority of problems. When a child becomes frustrated, aggressive, or disruptive, they separate the child and remain with him, speaking softly, until he's calm.

Parent/caregiver interaction: One of the neglected aspects of putting an infant or toddler in day care is the risk it poses to the parent's sense of confidence and self-esteem. For example, if a mother feels the new care-giver is having better success with her child, she may begin feeling unsure of herself. If she feels she's abandoned her child, she may become ridden with guilt. In either case, the mother's anxiety will translate into her inter-action with her child and set the stage for some potentially seri-ous problems. In a good day-care setting, the staff is sensitive to any adjustment problems the parent or parents may be having and will provide the understanding and support necessary to help them through this transition. In the final analysis, the in-teraction between parent and care-giver is every bit as impor-tant as the interaction between care-giver and toddler. When shopping for day care, therefore, you should trust your instincts and first impressions concerning the director and staff. Did you get a good feeling from them? Did they seem genuine? Did you like them? Did they seem warm and personable as opposed to "all business"?

Emancipation Is a Two-way Street

If you are reading carefully, you realize by now that, in com-ing down in favor of parent care during the first three years of life, I am not describing a model for overprotection or smother-ing. Quite the contrary, the parent who stays at home during his or her child's first three years of life provides a stable sense of trust and in so doing promotes greater independence. The se-cure child is able to emancipate much more quickly and suc-cessfully than the insecure child. By investing this time during the child's infancy and toddlerhood, the stay-at-home parent fosters self-sufficiency. The payoff comes around age three in the form of a child who is able to occupy himself for long peri-ods of time, is not demanding or whining, and is generally able to separate from his parents with ease. In the final analysis, therefore, this is a model for the successful emancipation of both parent *and* child.

With or For?

Listening, a year or so ago, to a radio talk show, I heard a woman who called herself a feminist make the claim that women of her mother's generation were "victims" of "enslavement" to housework, husband, and children. I found this most interesting, because lots of women of her mother's generation—which is also my mother's generation—attend my talks around the country, and I often ask them about their child-rearing years. They consistently report that not only were they content with their "lot in life," but they also pursued interests of their own outside of housework, husband, and children. Despite political and professional barriers, these were women who thought of themselves as whole.

Shortly after hearing this radio interview, I gave a talk in Omaha. Afterward, a woman approached me and asked what I thought about her decision to stay home with her children as, she said, her mother had done. I took a bold chance and said, "I don't believe your mother stayed home *with* you."

She visibly bristled and shot back, "She did too! What do you know?"

"I know that if your mother was anything like my mother," I answered, "and anything like the dozens of other mothers I came to know during my childhood, she got you fed and dressed in the morning and sent you outside to play, perhaps even with instructions not to come home, unless you had an emergency, until lunch."

Her eyes widened, her body language relaxed, and her mouth dropped open in amazement. She said, "Well, come to think of it, that's exactly what she did."

"Right!" I said, "Then she wasn't at home *with* you, she was home *for* you, and there is a world of difference. Your mother expected you to be as independent of her as she was of you. She didn't hover over you during the day, finding you things to do, driving you from one activity to another, making sure you were busy. She didn't measure her adequacy in terms of how much she did for her children. When it came to her relationship with her children, she was a very liberated woman, for sure."

She pondered this for a moment, then said, "So what you're saying is, if I choose to stay home, I must take just as good care of myself as I do my children."

Exactly, and more. I'm saying these supposedly unliberated women were our mothers only when we needed mothers. The rest of the time they were adult women, doing as they chose.

They were not at our beck and call, nor did they think the measure of a woman was how much she did for her children. They expected us to be independent, fight our own battles, occupy our own time, stand on our own two feet. They called themselves not "stay-at-home moms," but "housewives," thus referring to themselves as women whose primary relationships were with other adults, not children. The exceptions were privately called "overly protective" and "smothering" by their peers.

Women of that generation either bristle or laugh when I ask if, in retrospect, they think of themselves as victims. They were, they insist, committed. They viewed their work as essential to the conservation of both family and culture. And, I dare say, in the way they lived their lives, they demonstrated that it's possible to be liberated and not work outside the home.

The disingenuous attempt to discredit these women as role models is part of a larger attempt on the part of the self-appointed avant-garde to replace traditional values with nouveau values—ones that endure with ones spun from the whole cloth of rhetoric. If it succeeds, the sound we will hear will be that of our foremothers turning over in their graves.

Despite rhetoric to the contrary, the American family *worked* as well as could reasonably be expected when husbands were breadwinners and wives stayed home with the children. (It goes without saying that I'm speaking in general terms here.) Once upon a time, this was regarded as simply a logical and necessary division of responsibilities. Unfortunately, over time, this tradition gave rise to stereotypes that were debasing of the general capabilities of women. We began to confuse what women had and had not done with what they were and were not capable of doing. This confusion pumped adrenaline into the neofeminist movement and provided ideal opportunity for the movement to broaden its power base by convincing American women they were members of a victim class. According to the new feminist manifesto, a woman was not complete, and therefore not liberated, if she relegated herself to the role of housewife. Thus began the cultural devaluing of the traditional female role of full-time wife and mother. As women were seduced and intimidated by this insidiously antifamily agenda into putting their children into day care and entering the job force, the American family went into a precipitous state of decline. In the official language, the American family has simply been "changing" over the last thirty years. This is nothing but a euphemistic way of saying that for at least three decades, the American family has been in a steady state of decline, getting progressively weaker and weaker. And as the family goes, so goes the culture. In the final analysis, America is only as strong as its families are healthy. Restoring our domestic health, therefore, has less to do with raising or lowering taxes to create or eliminate this or that government program, and more to do with a reaffirmation of the traditional family values that were the backbone of this country since its inception. This is the stuff of the culture wars in which we are currently engaged.

Be advised that my interpretation of recent historical processes does not carry with it the recommendation that mothers should stay at home with their children while their husbands go to work. I am thoroughly convinced that a committed stay-at-home father is as capable of providing a properly responsive emotional environment for a young child as is a committed mother. Bonding studies have focused almost exclusively on the mother's role, but we are beginning to discover how important fathers are to their children's overall well-being. There is, for example, indication that children whose fathers are actively involved in their care are more outgoing and possess generally better social skills and are more accepting of challenge than children whose fathers are relatively uninvolved. In short, there is every reason to believe that infants and toddlers thrive well when their primary care is provided by loving fathers. The best of all possible worlds, of course, is one in which mom and dad share parenting responsibilities as equally as possible.

Questions?

Q *Our first child is twenty months. Two months ago, I went back to work and put her in a church day-care center. At first, Stephanie had difficulty separating from me. After a couple of weeks, the crying and clinging stopped, but now I'm more concerned than ever. In the morning, she tells me she doesn't want to go to the center. I'm very direct in telling her that she must go, but I always reassure her of my return. When we arrive at the center, she goes quietly into her classroom. When I come to take her home, however, she gets upset and tells me she wants to stay. When I pick her up, she begins to cry and doesn't usually calm down until we get home. Her teachers tell me it takes her a little time to get into the swing of things, but once she's "over the hump," she seems to enjoy being with the other children. What could be going on here, and how should I handle it?*

A My best guess is that Stephanie is trying to tell you, in the only way she can, that she needs more stability. She tells you in the morning that she doesn't want to go to day care. In other words, she prefers the stability and security of home. At this point, however, she accepts your direction and separates from you without protest. Then, just about the time she's managed to, as you put it, get "over the hump" and into the full swing of things at the center, you show up to take her home. She protests, you take her home, she makes that transition; then, the next day, the cycle starts all over again.

You already know that I feel Stephanie is a little young to be in full-time group care, but if your decision to return to work at this time is firm, then I'd suggest you look into daycare arrangements that wouldn't require such dramatic transitions. You might look into having someone come into your home to care for Stephanie. This type of care is generally more expensive than the other options, but as with any other product or service, you get what you pay for. An in-home provider would be able to give Stephanie the individual attention she needs at this stage of her development, and Stephanie wouldn't have to "shift gears" twice a day. You might, in this context, have Stephanie spend one or two mornings a week at a "Mother's Morning Out" program or toddler play group so that she has some opportunity for interaction with other children.

If in-home care isn't affordable or feasible, then my next suggestion would be that you try to find a family home day-care setting for Stephanie. The relative familiarity of a home setting might be more compatible with her emotional needs at this point. You'd probably experience fewer problems if you waited to put her into group care until she was at least three.

Q *I've just returned from another disastrous morning at a three-morning-a-week preschool class I attend with my twenty-eight-month-old son. The program is organized around learning experiences designed to stimulate intelligence, imagination, and other developmental skills. While the other children sit calmly paying attention to the teacher, I chase my child, trying to keep him under control. The class only lasts an hour, but when it's over, I'm ready for a nap. How can I get him to mind me during this time?*

A I don't, for the life of me, understand why you're attending a preschool program *with* your son. If the purpose is to teach you how to teach your child, I can assure you that twenty-eight-month-old children don't need any "teaching." They need environments that encourage exploration and experimentation, and parents who read to them a lot, play with them a little, and supervise them well. A preschool child's imagination and intellect will grow to full capacity without being artificially "stimulated" with contrived "learning experiences."

Besides, don't you need a break? At this age, a part-time preschool program serves only two purposes: giving the child some social experience and giving the front-line parent some time away from the child. In this type of program, a child begins to learn how to play constructively with other children as well as how to be independent of mommy. I'd encourage you to enroll him in a morning program that accomplishes both goals. I suspect you're paying a lot of money for a program that's more "show" than "go."

Q *I've always heard the most important thing working parents can give their children is quality time. My husband and I both work full-time (I went back to work four months ago), and our almost-three-year-old spends the day in an excellent, church-operated child development center where, because of the support of the congregation, the child/staff ratio is lower than at any other program in the city. After we get home, change clothes, and have dinner, there isn't a lot of time left before our daughter's bedtime. What's the best way to bring quality into the little time we have together in the evening?*

A In the first place, the most important thing two working parents can give their children is a strong marriage. I'm not saying quality time spent with your child isn't important; I'm saying it's more important that you spend quality time with one another. Keep in mind that, at this age, you should be focused on moving your daughter out of the center of attention in your family, and positioning yourselves at the center of her attention.

If, five out of seven days a week, you only have three hours in which to be a family, that's all the more reason for you to keep your family priorities in order during that time. To be sure, a child needs attention from parents, and the younger the child, the more attention is needed. But parents also need time together as husband and wife, and children need to see their parents spending this time together. A child cannot learn that her parents' marriage is the "keystone" relationship in the family if, whenever they're together as a family, they act almost exclusively from within the roles of mother and father.

Furthermore, you should, by now, be expecting your daughter to be more responsible for keeping herself occupied. By the time a child is three, she should be able to play independently for most of the evening, making only occasional requests of her parents. Parents, on the other hand, are responsible for encouraging that independence by providing her with creative playthings, giving her guidance as needed, reinforcing her accomplishments, and occasionally playing with her, but not to the extent that they become her playmates.

As your daughter's bedtime approaches, it makes good sense to spend time preparing her for this transition. A period of closeness, during which you bathe her, read to her, and talk quietly to her for a few minutes before tucking her in and leaving her room is definitely needed, but evening after entire evening of two-on-one will prevent the transition to parent-centeredness that is so critical at this stage. Naturally, the weekends will find you spending more time with her, simply because there is more time to spend. Nonetheless, you still need to find plenty of opportunity for "marriage-time."

Q *We are teachers of two-year-olds in a child development center. At this writing, the ten children in our group range from twenty-six to thirty-two months. Our problem is Randolph, a sweet and loving thirty-month-old who will not join in group activities and generally goes limp whenever we tell him to do something, like pick up toys. He's not shy, because he's very social in free play situations where there's little, if any, structure. When we have an organized activity, however, he will usually move to another area of the classroom and do his own thing. If we coax, he ignores us. If we try to physically make him join the group, he becomes a wet dishrag. Mind you, he's not disruptive, just uncooperative. We've tried everything except ignoring him, which is impossible because we don't want the other children thinking they have permission to follow suit. We also feel an obligation to make sure Randolph benefits from being in the program, not to mention that his parents get their money's worth. Do you have any suggestions?*

A I understand your reluctance to ignore Randolph, but if you've pulled out all the stops and nothing has worked, then perhaps ignoring is all you can do. But don't despair! In the long run, ignoring just may turn out to be the most strategic of all approaches.

As I've said before, it's difficult, at best, to *correct* the behavior of a child this age. First, two-year-olds do not readily make the connection between misbehavior and consequences. As a result, even the most well-thought-out "punishment" may have no lasting impact at all. Furthermore, as anyone who's ever tried to get a two-year-old to sit in a chair knows, the attempt to enforce consequences may only create more problems than it solves. Lastly, this age child has yet to acquire a highly coveted set of privileges. Disciplinary leverage is, therefore, lacking. For all these reasons, it's generally more realistic to think in terms of *containment* than *correction* when disciplining a two-year-old.

I suspect Randolph is feeding off the attention you've been giving these problems. By ignoring him when he separates himself from the group, by letting him do his own thing, you not only contain the problem to Randolph, but also starve it of fuel. If he's not successful at getting your attention, he may eventually run out of gas.

How do you explain this to the other children? By simply telling them, should they ask, "Randolph isn't going to join us, so we're going to read (or whatever) without him." If another child tries to join him, just be firm and unequivocal in bringing him back to the group. You don't need, in other words, to give an elaborate explanation or justification. You say so. That's all any other child needs to hear. Concerning your obligations to Randolph and his parents, fear not! I can assure you Randolph is benefiting from the program regardless of the level of his participation. In any case, he will get from the program what he's ready to get, and no more. Remember, you can't push a river.

Q *We are the grandparents of a very sweet but spoiled thirty-month-old whose parents recently won a week's vacation in Tahiti. They asked us to sit while they're away, which we're delighted to do. After we agreed, however, conditions began creeping into the discussion. We'd like to take him with us on an adventure of sorts, but they don't want him away from home except for day trips. They are concerned he will suffer some sort of psychological trauma if he's not only separated from them, but his "security environment" (as they put it) as well. We discovered that he's never been left with anyone, not even for a few hours, and that his parents lie down with him every night until he's asleep. (They say they're only going to do this until he's older and more secure.) Do you have any advice for us?*

A This is exactly the sort of thing parents of this generation have been conditioned to agonize over. Granted, your grandson's parents seem to be agonizing a bit more than most, but this hypersensitivity to the imagined emotional frailty of children is typical of today's parents, the first generation to believe that psychologists and other supposed "experts" (like yours truly!) know more about raising children than do grandparents.

In truth, human children are extremely resilient. If a thirty-month-old is basically secure, then being left in the care of a familiar and competent person—grandparent or otherwise—for a week is not going to be disruptive. Furthermore, whether or not the child is in his "security environment" during this time is immaterial.

Keep in mind, however, that in this case we may not be talking about an entirely secure child. Sleeping with (even lying down with) a two-year-old does *not* promote security. Nor does never leaving the child in the care of others. In both cases, the separation issue is being avoided. This age child cannot feel a complete sense of security unless his parents have given him permission to stand on his own, venture away from them, experience autonomy, be his own person. To do that—to be given, in other words, permission to grow up—the child must know it's okay to be separated from his parents. He must know that when they go away, they always come back.

Avoiding separation hobbles the growth of autonomy and, therefore, promotes insecurity. Furthermore, the longer one waits to confront and resolve this critical developmental issue, the more difficult and painful it will be for all concerned. This situation provides an ideal opportunity for starting down the road to resolution. For the sake of a smooth transition, you should arrive at the parents' home one or two days prior to their departure. During that time, it should be business as usual. No mention should be made of the fact the parents are leaving. A buildup of any sort will simply sensitize your grandson that something is about to happen that's making his parents act very different. His parents' uncomfortable behavior will increase the likelihood of clinging and screaming when the moment for "good-bye" arrives.

On the morning of his parents' departure, say, "Guess what? You're going in the car with Grandma and Grandpa today!" After he's dressed and his parents say their (very brief) good-byes, put him in the car and off you go! When, later, he asks questions about his parents, you answer them simply, honestly, and matter-of-factly. When he asks you to lie down with him at night, do what your common sense tells you is right. In the final analysis, it's his parents' job to resolve that issue, not yours. And I'd advise them not to waste a night in resolving it once they return from Tahiti.

"A Final Word or Two"

The worst of times, the best of times. That description fits no other stage of human growth and development as well as it does toddlerhood. Sometimes terrible, but always lovable, the toddler careens through this eighteen or so months of life in constant search of answers to "what is it?" and "how does it work?" The compelling nature of these questions spells lots of work for parents. The trick is to find the line between allowing the child the freedom needed to discover what makes the world "tick" and keeping the child from getting into trouble; the freedom to begin the discovery of who he is and is capable of becoming while at the same time establishing the understanding that parents are in charge. And a fine line it is. Which means, dear reader-parent, you are going to make mistakes, and plenty of 'em. You are going to lose your patience, overreact, underreact, and fail to react until far too late. You are not a perfect being; therefore, you will never be a perfect parent. You won't even get close. Bad news, eh?

Ah, but the good news is that children are extremely resilient, much more so than their parents, usually. It follows that children generally recover from their parents' mistakes far more quickly than their parents recover from the anxiety and guilt of making them. Have you ever noticed how forgiving little children are? They seem to realize that their parents' mistakes are nothing more than a consequence of being human, slightly amplified by the tendency to take children much too seriously, and that their parents have great difficulty forgiving themselves. So, just when you can't feel any worse about some parenting "crime" you committed, your little one crawls up on your lap and snuggles in for a hug, as if to say, "There, there, now everything's still all right in my life, so take it easy on yourself, okay?"

And the further good news is that if you've taken the time to read this book, you're not the type of parent who's going to make the same mistakes over and over again. You're going to learn from them, and as time passes, you're going to become a better and better parent. You'll never be perfect, but you'll always be the only mother or father your child will ever want. So take that as a vote of confidence and do your best, because your best is always and forever going to be good enough.

Enjoy!

Index

About the Author

Family psychologist John Rosemond is director of the Center for Affirmative Parenting (CAP), headquartered in Gastonia, North Carolina. CAP is a national parent resource center whose aim is to provide parents with commonsensical parenting advice as well as whatever guidance they need as they strive to endow their children with what John refers to as the "Three R's"—respect, responsibility, and resourcefulness. Toward that end, CAP provides workshops and educational presentations for parents and professionals who work with children. CAP also has available print, audio, and audiovisual materials on parenting and child development.

Since 1978, John has written a nationally syndicated family column which currently appears in over one hundred newspapers across the United States and Canada. He is also the regularly featured parenting columnist for *Better Homes and Gardens* magazine and *Hemispheres*, United Air Lines' in-flight magazine.

Making the "Terrible" Twos Terrific! is John's fourth book for Andrews and McMeel. His first, *John Rosemond's Six-Point Plan for Raising Happy, Healthy Children* (1989), which *Esquire* magazine called "refreshingly reactionary," has been a best-seller since 1990. *Ending the Homework Hassle* (1990) and *Parent Power!* (1991) followed to equally excellent sales and reviews.

In 1981, John was selected "Professional of the Year" by the Mecklenburg County Mental Health Association of Charlotte, North Carolina. In 1986, he was presented with the Alumni Achievement Award by his alma mater, Western Illinois University.

Throughout the year, John is in considerable demand as a public speaker. His humorous, provocative parenting presentations and workshops have drawn consistently high marks from parent and professional groups all over the country.

Last, but by no means least, John is husband to Willie and father to Eric, twenty-four, and Amy, twenty-one. Eric is a corporate pilot currently flying for a corporate charter company. Amy is finishing at the University of North Carolina, Chapel Hill, where she is majoring in communications and basketball worship.

Anyone interested in obtaining information about John's presentations, workshops, or parenting materials can do so by writing The Center for Affirmative Parenting, P.O. Box 4124, Gastonia, North Carolina, or calling (704) 864-1012.